Endorsements

"Love the book! Masterful, timely, and life changing for the journeyer and their loved ones. Should be required reading for everyone. Chapter 7 is worth the price of the book! It takes the unknown, the fear out of the dying process and lets you know what to expect."

Dr. Lin Morel
Trauma Consultant, Author

"On this planet with a plenitude of diverse cultures and traditions, we all share a few common characteristics. We are, without exception, born onto a one-way street leading to a certain ending. And most of us do not receive an owner's manual on how to pass through the stages of this journey. This beautiful book places in our hands, and hearts, the tools critical for gracefully traveling the end of road years, whether for ourselves or a loved one. It is a must read for seniors and all who love seniors."

Jan T. Adams, MD, Physician and Writer

"Bravo for this important guidebook easing you into your golden years. Easy-to-follow steps masterfully detailed in this exceptional book help you navigate your future with peaceful awareness. Positive emotions engaged, you feel prepared, safe, and content on your journey. It's a joy to recommend this essential and uplifting information to my coaching clients."

Dr. Judy Krings
Positive Psychology Coach and Author

"Terrific road map for how to navigate your retirement years. It covers far more than end of life planning—everything from forgiveness to care choices to estate planning and beyond. You will gain confidence to take charge of your life, ask the right questions, and live your life to the fullest. You will realize new options and gain a sense of peace, returning to this book many times, whether you are caring for a loved one or planning your own Last Journey."

Sherri Marini, Certified Estate Planner
Legacy Financial Strategies, Inc.

"Residents in retirement communities experience a sense of camaraderie and comfort in realizing they can actualize their dreams and have a safe place to discuss and work through end-of-life details. This wonderful book shows them how to get from where they may be today to where they want to be."

Sam Carrillo, Executive Director
The Stratford Retirement Community

"At some point in every senior's life, fundamental questions become pressing: Will my resources last as long as I do? And how about those decisions I need to make sooner rather than later? This comprehensive resource takes readers by the hand through the questions they have thought of, but not yet considered. Real-life details in this book will leave readers far better prepared for the years ahead."

Judy Keene, Writer

The Last Journey

The Last Journey

A Road Map for Ending-of-Days

Carole Ann Drick, RN, PhD
Lynn Keegan, RN, PhD
K. Penney Sanders, PhD

The Last Journey: A Road Map For Ending-of-Days

Copyright © 2022 by:
Carole Ann Drick; Lynn Keegan; K. Penney Sanders

All rights reserved. No part of this book may be used or reproduced by any means, graphic, electronic, or mechanical, including photocopying, recording, taping, or by any information storage retrieval system without the written permission of the publisher, except in the case of brief quotations embodied in critical articles and reviews.

ISBN: 979-8-9868130-0-4
Library of Congress Control Number: 2022915495

Cover Design by: Bill Van Nimwegen

Sacred Life Publishers™
SacredLife.com
Printed in the United States of America

Dedication

*This book is respectfully and lovingly dedicated
with deep appreciation to you the reader and your family
wherever you are in your Last Journey.*

Contents

Endorsements

Dedication vii

Author's Note xiii

1. **The Journey Begins** 1
   Where We Are Now and Why It Matters 1

2. **Pack Your Luggage Lightly** 5
   The Art of Reminiscing 5
   Stories and Beliefs 6
   The Forgiveness Factor 9
   Becoming Peaceful 11

3. **Your Journey, Many Roads;**
   Not All of Them Are Paved 15
   Terms for Your Journey: The Jargon 16
   Considering Ending-of-Days Care Costs 18
   Housing Choices 19
       Staying In Your Own Home 20
       Independent Living Facilities 22
       Assisted Living Facilities 23
       Skilled Nursing Facilities/
           Nursing Homes 24
       Hospice 27
   A Frequent Ending-of-Days Scenario 29

4. **Road Maps and Papers for Your Journey** 33
   Power of Attorney 34

    Advanced Directives..35
    Physicians Order in Life Sustaining
        Treatment (POLST)...36
    Living Wills..37
    Last Will or Testament..39
    Other Documents for Your Journey 39
        Community Property Agreements......................39
        Trusts 40
    Additional Road Map Instructions...............................42
        Final Arrangement Preferences 43
        Your Obituary in Your Own Words 43
        Data for Your Death Certificate 44

5. Saying Goodbye 47
    When, Where, How, to Whom, and Why
        To Say Goodbye 47
    Who Do You Want with You at the Ending-of-Days?.....49
    Sharing Grief and Loss in Your Goodbyes........................50
    Leaving Instructions 51
        Looking Your Best..52
        Choosing Your Travel Outfit 52
        Final Resting Preferences......................................54
        Prepared/Pre-funded Arrangements 54
    Do You Want to Plan Your Own Funeral? 56
    Considering Relatives..66

6. You Have Options 69
    Are We Consciousness or Solely a Physical Body?..........70
    Graceful Aging All Along the Way 70
    Experiencing Grief and Loss..72
        Grief and Relief 73
        Anticipatory Grief—The Parallel Journey................74

  Antidote for Anticipatory Grief 75
  Anticipatory Relief - The Journey Ends and Begins. 79
 Lost? Ask the Right Questions.................................... 80

7. Arriving at Your Destination.................................... 85
 Your Ending-of-Days Process................................... 85
 The Day Before You Die and Why Doing What
  Really Matters Is Important 86
 The Big "D" Itself.. 87
 The Most Personal Journey 88
 The Physical Process of Your Body Closing Down 88
 As Your Ending-of-Days Comes Nearer 89
 Mental, Social, and Psychological Changes...................... 89
 The Last Days 90
  Appetite and Dehydration... 90
  Wakefulness and Sleep.. 91
  Breathing 92
  Blood Pressure, Temperature,
   and Circulation 94
  Senses 94
  And on The Last Day 96
  Summary 96

8. The Big "N"- Next.. 99
 What Happens After My Journey Ends?........................... 99
 What Happens to My Body?... 100
 What About My Loved Ones After I Am Gone?............. 102
  Allowing the Presence of Grief 104
  Becoming the Watcher.. 105
  The Watcher 106
  When the Tears Come 106

The Power of Your Breath to Assist You,
    the Traveler 107
What Happens to the Things I Left Behind? 109
    Giving Away and Reorganizing 109
    Home Death 109
    The Last Time 110
    Holiday Celebrations 111
    Remembering 112
    Maintaining Hope and Faith 113
    Getting Stuck and Unstuck 114
What Happens the First Year After My Passing? 115
A Rite of Passage 115

9. There's No Such Place as Faraway 117
    Our Last Message for You 121

Quote 123

About the Authors 125
    Carole Ann Drick 126
    Lynn Keegan 127
    Penney Sanders 128

Author's Note

*The art of living well and the art of dying well
are one and the same.*
~ Epicurus
(341-270 BCE)

The Last Journey of our life is akin to the first, our birth and beginning of life. For many, this trek is not necessarily an easy one. Gestation, childbirth, and the early weeks of beginning life, for both the giver (mother) and receiver of life (child), can be filled with both discomfort and fear as well as anticipation and excitement. All aspects of our humanness: body, mind, and spirit are engaged. On the other hand, there can be, and often is, a sense of overwhelming relief and exhilarating joy when the deed is accomplished, the child has been birthed.

What you already know is the ending-of-days differs. The dying process consists of similar feelings and physical challenges. This is the reason we three senior professionals, schooled and clinically experienced in this final episode of life, present ourselves to you with this guidebook containing years of both practical and scholastic wisdom.

This guide offers you a road map to help traverse this journey; to make your passage easier and less burdensome. We offer a clear, simple, step-by-step approach, and like all travel, is across many different subjects and experiences designed to prepare you for this one-of-a-kind Last Journey. As you read you will discover both perennial wisdom and contemporary thinking to assist your understanding and navigating this, one of the most personal times in your life.

As with all expeditions, some of the terrain can, at times, feel bumpy and challenging. And yet, you already have the wisdom, skills, and experience from many of your life experiences that you can draw upon to assist you on this, your Last Journey. As you follow along you will discover just how many of your own previous experiences you can use.

Our goal is to assist you in experiencing your ending-of-days by enriching your thoughts and giving you a solid, workable plan to prepare for one of the most meaningful times in your life, the Last Journey.

    Carole Ann
    Lynn
    Penney

1

The Journey Begins

Every journey has a beginning, middle and an end. Your life is exclusive starting with your birth, all your experiences across your lifetime and now approaching your ending-of-days. This has been a one-of-a-kind lifetime. And now it's time to continue that valued life as you journey into your ending-of-days. Only now, traveling forward into this unknown, we will go together.

Where We Are Now and Why It Matters

Our population, culture and care costs are changing rapidly. The United States population is aging.

By 2030:
1. the number of Americans aged sixty-five and older will more than double to seventy-one million older people
2. the nation's health care spending is projected to increase by 25 percent due to aging Americans

3. older adults will comprise roughly 20 percent of the US population

Here is the challenge. As our population is getting older in larger numbers, at the same time, inflation is causing the prices of goods and services to explode upwards.

Add to this the probability that an American who reaches age sixty-five will survive to age ninety. This figure has nearly doubled over the past forty years—from just 14 percent of sixty-five-year-olds in 1960 to 25 percent at present. By 2050, statisticians anticipate that 40 percent of sixty-five-year-olds are likely to reach age ninety. While our living may extend another twenty-five years, there will also be increasing disabil-ities and chronic diseases. As a result, costs for ending-of-days care are increasing exponentially and will continue with no end in sight.

This is serious and it comes at the end of your journey. You have a choice to be a lemming and tumble off the cliff with all the other lemmings or you can begin to make plans for your future decisions and costs. To be foretold is to be forearmed. In other words, you can begin to take charge of what you want and what you don't want.

You are waking up to the need for thoughtful considera-tion of financial costs at ending-of-days. For example, diagnostic imaging (frequently referred to as a scan) is used more frequently even in people with end stage, advanced cancers. As reported in the Journal of the National Cancer Institute, the use of scanning now averages 9.7 scans per patient despite limited survival times.

So, ask yourself, do you want or need all this expensive care at ending-of-days? Or do you want to use your money for peaceful, compassionate care and care givers in a holistic, comfortable setting? This is your journey; you get to decide.

1 — The Journey Begins

One thing you know for sure: *all* of us will outlive our physical body. No exceptions. The more we know and prepare for this, the better. By facing death proactively, you can come to greater peace with your physical mortality and lay the groundwork for your own ending-of-days needs and expenses. This means collecting the information so you know your options and can be proactive and make wise decisions. We all come from very different financial and family backgrounds. There are no wrong decisions; what is wrong is *not* making the decisions.

Are you and your family ready financially for your Last Journey? More than half of all workers and their spouses have less than $25,000 in household savings and investments. Because women generally earn less than men and have a longer life expectancy, women are at greater economic risk. When women end up older and alone—whether it's widowed, divorced, or never married—many risk falling into a higher level of poverty. On average, approximately 20 percent of elderly women are classified as "in poverty."

Others save and plan for retirement and ending-of-days and then are faced with unexpected inflation. Their savings do not cover their needs. Some turn to their children for help. Unfortunately, not everyone has family, wants to, or can live with their children.

There are so many factors that affect each older adult's financial situation. American Association of Retired Persons, or AARP, reports 22.3 percent of women and 12.5 percent of men aged fifty plus live alone. This startling statistic reflects the change in our family structure over the last fifty years.

Additionally, there are over six million adults with Alzheimers and other Dementias, with almost half of those having no identifiable caregiver. Their care expenses generally fall to the government programs, Medicare and more specifically Medicaid.

Remember—you are one of the fortunate ones. You are becoming aware of long-range planning and can do something about your future care and quality of life. It is never too late to look at your options and make the best decisions based upon what you have. And so, your journey begins with you reflecting on who you are, where you have been, and your remaining days ahead and what you want and need in this time. This journey is all about you as you are one of a kind.

> *Dear loved ones and friends,*
>
> *On my goodness. I am ready to begin this journey, and I haven't even started. I just wanted to let you know that this might be what I have been looking for and I didn't know it. Here is a book that will take me step-by-step through this experience. It has already answered some questions for me and that I can take my time and take it all in. I didn't realize how many choices I had. To be honest, I never realized how special I was. Oh, probably, you all would tell me that, but I never really let it in. Somehow hearing or reading it from a stranger all makes sense. I'm so pleased you are there to share this with me.*
>
> *More later,*
> *M*

2

Pack Your Luggage Lightly

We have all been young; we will all grow old. Wherever we find our self is just the perfect place to be because that is where you are. Now wherever, and however, you find yourself consider how you might continue to prepare for this one-of-a-kind journey. Let's begin packing your suitcase by keeping your luggage light. You won't need clothes, shoes, toiletries, swimsuit, or even snacks. Rather let's include love, joy, peace, and forgiveness, then close your suitcase after adding memories and reminiscences of years gone by. Your suitcase is light so there is plenty of room to add important things as your journey progresses.

The Art of Reminiscing

Reminiscing is a natural process of describing past events and adventures either to family, friends, or ourselves. There's an art to reminiscing. Many people keep personal journals or write annual holiday letters to share their lives with others. Think of how much time you spend talking about your plans, goals, abilities, successes, letdowns, and failures. These are all forms of reminiscing that focus on the immediate past. Today in some circles they would be called "my story" or "drama." Many people spend part of their elder days telling others about their life. It may seem to others as if they are saying, see how important I am and how important my life is. This is not the case, instead they are remembering their lives and when putting those memories into words in a conversation with another, it validates who they were, the valuable things they believed and accomplished; all factors in who you are. This offers an opportunity for others to also value and validate their life.

Another part of reminiscing is remembering childhood, schooling, your parents, your aspirations, your hopes, and dreams. This reflecting contains a deeper understanding of how one's life unfolded. It's seeing the patterns, twists, and turns that have brought you to this point in life. It is about being with the memories and seeing them for what they are, memories, and not getting caught up in the emotions surrounding them. There is a gentle smile of realization of that was then and this is now. Both are good and both have elements of love and disappointment.

Reminiscing is about separating out the past from the present and living in this time. When we live in the past, we are unable to embrace life and all it has for us in this moment. So, pack some of these fun positive memories in your suitcase.

Stories and Beliefs

Our beliefs and values, based on our stories, are the foundation we have built that reinforces our life's journey; they help us find meaning and purpose. They build hope and reinforce the need to take the steps toward our goals and aspirations. They show how we have put effort into our live to achieve a goal. They can reinforce our desire to keep moving forward. Our stories serve as benchmarks along the way to help us recognize our choices, successes, strengths, areas to improve and refine our goals. Our stories provide a feeling of connection with ourselves, others, and life itself.

For some people, their stories and beliefs may hold them back. Sometimes our memories are looked upon as things lost and never to be replaced again: a significant year in high school, being on a sport's team, a first love, a perfect birthday or a one day of fame . . . .

We have a choice to use our stories and beliefs as building blocks to move us forward or to use them to keep us stagnated or stuck. Moving forward means that we recognize that life is lived in this moment. The past is a memory and no longer real. We can, however, capture the joy when we share it. It is never too late to have a happy and fulfilled life.

Stories are also part of an oral tradition that began before the written word. As a result, they became an important part of a family's history that was passed from one generation to the next. Many grandparents are especially good at carrying on this oral tradition as they recall their children's growing up. This becomes increasingly fun when they tell these stories to their grandchildren as their own children look on sometimes in awe of their parents' memories. They may recall when they took their first steps and couldn't stop and ran into the wall, or learning to ride a bike and in the process ran into a tree—the only tree in the yard.

One family began their oral tradition with their children as they told stories of when the children were young, and they would all laugh. Then the parents would tell stories about themselves when they were young, too. Soon, the young children were telling stories about themselves and laughing; then stories were expanded to include grandparents and friends. These stories became increasingly relevant in strengthening the family bonds as the family came together for holidays as well as for watchful waiting during the ending-of-days.

A friend had the opportunity to ask her mother and father to tell her stories about growing up on their family farms. Each of their stories, rich in memories, explained a lot and helped her to understand and appreciate where she came from and who she was.

This is what she learned. Her mother's family was poor; yet living on the family farm, they always ate well. She was the second of six children. She had one pair of shoes that she wore on Sunday and boots for winter. Both at home and at her one-room school, she went barefoot. She had two dresses, one for Sunday and one everyday dress. When the everyday dress was being washed, she either stayed in bed or, when young, she ran around in her underpants. Eventually, she went to college, majored in home economics, and after graduation became an incredible seamstress in addition to teaching high school home economics. This explained why both her and her mother had so many beautiful clothes and how the meals she prepared were both nutritious and full of love.

Her father was the fourth of five boys, and got a lot of teasing from his older brothers. Because of this teasing, he retained a strong gentle humor that was passed down to his children and grandchildren. Growing up on the family farm he learned early to be self-reliant and how to repair equipment with the tools and materials that they had on the farm. As a second generation "off the boat" from Germany, his work ethic was strong, doing an honest day's work for an honest day's pay. My friend vividly remembers her dad's hands, which were soft. He was a farm boy tall, strong, and quickly took to wrestling at college, and became the first in the family to complete both college and a master's degree.

This friend's brother had the foresight to record their father speaking about his childhood. Regrettably, he didn't get to record their mother.

Fortunately, my friend talked with both of her parents several times about their childhood and growing up. She enjoyed this special time together, but didn't realize how meaningful this experience was until she was older.

The Forgiveness Factor

One of the things that often occurs as we grow older is a growing sense of the importance of forgiveness. Learning to forgive may be an unconscious realization of aging. Life teaches us that forgiving takes a lot less energy. Forgiving can be a learned experience and is essential to a full rich life and peaceful death.

Feeling guilty for past actions or assigning blame often results in misery, depression and/or anger. Both emotions are destructive to the body, coloring our feelings about other things, and robbing us of the energy to enjoy life. Additionally, negative feelings silently deprive us of energy and time; time for creating loving relationships and focusing on our ending-of-days aspirations and our goals.

As we begin to forgive ourself, in turn we can forgive others. Both can be challenging; both are necessary. Forgiving begins by letting go of the self-blame for past actions. The underlying ability to forgive our self is to become honest as to what worked or didn't work in our life. Self-blame is often a challenge that can involve tears and disappointment that we didn't meet our own expectations. And yet, with this realization comes a new freedom. It is like a heavy weight has been lifted from our chest; we can breathe again freely and more effortlessly.

One client from Oklahoma, who prided herself as being non-judgmental, shared that she was out walking in the fields behind the farm, and had the realization that she could forgive others but not herself. She had to be strong and always in control. As she had the realization that this behavior no longer supported her, she felt the intense hardness in her heart soften and she smiled in relief and shedding tears of thankfulness.

Forgiveness also involves heartfelt listening to what others are saying to you. One way people inadvertently hurt others is by simply not listening to them. This ending-of-days listening is a deep listening; not just to the words but listening from a deep inner place. It is sharing with the other person how you feel and experience this inner emotion. This is a place of connectedness that is greater than words and is the essence of empathy. In this deep inner place, you can let go of your judgments and expectations about them, their life, and their actions. You can open wide your heart to this place of understanding, honoring, and accepting them as they are.

An older gentleman, in Pennsylvania, was sitting with his daughter in the backyard at sunset listening to the family indoors laughing and playing a game. His daughter began to speak slowly and softly about her feelings regarding his being away working for much of her childhood and how much this hurt her, feeling unloved and uncared for by him. He didn't know if it was the evening quietness or what, but he felt his heart open. He could feel her pain and shared his longing to be with her more in her growing up. And, in that moment, they came together and sat quietly in a deeper space beyond words. Their connection grew deeper, allowing a new feeling of love, respect, and caring.

When living your life from a place of forgiveness, you find yourself in a new space of growing in unconditional love. You begin to ask; how can I criticize another while expecting others to accept where I am? When living the answer to this question, you begin to experience more love, peace, abundance, and joy. These are the gifts of unconditional love that are given as you continue releasing and letting go of anything and everything that causes even a moment of hesitation, fear, anger, or resentment. These are the gifts of forgiveness.

A wise sage was once asked, "What is Anger?" He thought for a moment then gave a simple answer, "Anger is a punishment you give to yourself for someone else's mistake." These wise words are key to offering forgiveness to others and thereby, healing to yourself.

Becoming Peaceful

Becoming peaceful is not something that you suddenly wake up with in the morning. Rather, it must be practiced repeatedly in each situation that comes in your life. A young mother tells the story that when she moved far away from home as a new bride, she prayed for peace. After a few months, she shared this prayer with her mother who became silent for a few moments. The mother then softly said, "Beth Ann, how do you think you will get peace?"

Becoming peaceful is a gift of your unconditional loving. As such the only place you can express unconditional love is here, right now. As you make a commitment to yourself to begin practicing living more in this moment, you start to embrace the gifts of peace and love that can come to everyone including you. It is never too late to begin to live a peaceful life.

Relaxation, meditation, or for many, prayer, are all excellent ways to become peaceful and increasingly being in the here and now. We can only relax, meditate, or pray in the present moment. One way that many people discover staying in the moment is through the power of their breath. Think about it; your breath is always with you, so it is accessible. You are already breathing, so there is nothing you need to add or learn. It goes unnoticed to other people so you can focus on your breathing at any place or time, even during a conversation. Your brain can only focus on one thing at a time so when you are focusing on your breathing and feeling the air going gently in and out, your mind cannot think about the past or the future. You can breathe and listen to a conversation or observe what is going on around you. This is powerful and as you begin to practice this; you will notice that you can begin to hear on a deeper level and you begin to become more perceptive and gentler with your responses.

Listening and observing in this moment means that your responses can come from an interior place rather than from a fearful, blaming mind. What have you got to lose? Try it. The three things that are required to be successful with your breath grounding you are: practice, practice, practice.

Your bags are packed so let's continue this one-of-a-kind journey. Celebrate your life with each step in this new final adventure known as ending-of-days.

Hi again,

Just a quick note. I tried the breathing, and it works. Never thought something so simple could help me so much. I just laughed and I'm going to use this for sure.
M

3

Your Journey, Many Roads Not All of Them Are Paved

Like any other journey—whether by train, plane, or car—there may be a redirection or change of plans. Your ending-of-days journey will be no exception. Rather than the predictable Interstate, your journey at times may take a back road filled with detours and, yes, some potholes. The important thing about this is you already know how to navigate the unexpected detours in your life. You have done this many times and in many different situations. You make small adjustments all during the day to hurry up, slow down, or cancel an activity. You already have the basic skills.

Let's describe some of these detours, which include possibly relocating from your home to a care facility as your care needs or other circumstances change. Also included are some of the realities of the related costs of ending-of-days care. But first let's take a brief look at the health care terminology or jargon that you are likely to hear during your Last Journey.

Selecting a care facility is like traveling in a foreign country: new location, different foods, and a different language. To make the journey, you need to understand the language of your destination. It is called "jargon" because it is very specific to the caregiving world in which you are traveling.

Terms for Your Journey: The Jargon

The following are the common health care terms that most people hear on their journey. More specific jargon depends upon your unique situation.

Activities of Daily Living (ADLs)

Your ability to do your activities is assessed by several methods. The most commonly used method is the Katz Index.

ADLs are:
- ability to walk and transfer yourself out of a bed or chair
- personal care (brush your teeth and hair) and ability to shower without assistance
- toileting: getting on/off toilet and personal cleanliness
- dressing yourself (no point reductions for wearing checks and stripes but appropriateness is a factor)
- feeding yourself (a clothing protector [bib] is allowed)

The ability to do your ADLs is factored in any residential placement.

Assisted Living Facility (ALF)

Assisted living facilities are designed for seniors who need *some* assistance with their day-to-day tasks. There is meal service (dining rooms), housekeeping services, and some assistance with activities of daily living (ADLs) including medication management.

As care needs increase, facilities assess care points at a dollar amount per point. Be aware of these fees as you review the appropriateness of an ALF.

Assisted living allows for more independent living while offering services and emergency support.

Certified Nurse Assistant (CNA)

Both ALFs and SNFs are staffed by CNAs who deliver direct care to facility residents. They work under the supervision of a nurse and help with many of the physical needs of the residents.

Instrumental Activities of Daily Living (IADLs)

These are the activities that are essential to your living independently, either in your own home or in a senior community. A Katz Index is used to also measure IADLs.

These more complex activities include:
- home chores: cleaning, laundry
- money management: check writing, bill paying
- meal preparation
- medication management
- using the telephone, computer, or other devices

Performance of both ADLs and IADLs are part of assessing and maintaining independence.

MEDICAID

This program is a federal-state partnership designed for low-income people, regardless of age. Medicaid benefits vary from state-to-state and there are very specific income guidelines for becoming part of the program.

MEDICARE

Medicare is a federal government insurance program. It serves people over age sixty-five regardless of income. There are some younger, disabled adults who are on Medicare. Participants pay a monthly fee that is income-based. There is Medicare A that covers hospital costs and Part B that covers other medical costs such as doctor visits.

Skilled Nursing Facility (SNF)

Also known as a nursing home or a care home. These facilities offer the highest level of care and are for the most seriously ill or incapacitated. Twenty-four hour nursing care and medication management are provided. These often have a rehab division.

Note: While going to a SNF for rehab is short-term (under 100 days), when you go for skilled nursing care, this is generally a long-term arrangement.

Considering Ending-of-Days Care Costs

Many of you may remember the TV programs of the 60s and 70s. *Marcus Welby, MD* or *Leave it to Beaver*? They reflected the "typical life" in America. It was a simple life with simple solutions; Dr. Welby made home visits. Our life today is far more complicated with technology that was not even imagined then.

So were the costs for health care and ending-of-days simple; people had extended families and one usually died at home.

In contrast, today the cost of caring for seniors is major public policy and a critical health care concern. Care costs for someone sixty-five plus are three-to-five times greater than care costs for someone younger than sixty-five. This makes sense as younger people tend to be healthier with fewer health care concerns. Yet, being older and probably wiser, you can make a difference here as you reflect on your health care now and picture what you would like in the future. Where to start?

Consider beginning with this first step: reflect on your attitude regarding your ending-of-days and what you expect or would certainly like. What kind of care do you prefer—one of life at any cost or the security and contentment in being supported, comfortable and loved? This is a pivotal question that can ease your decision-making process as you continue on your journey.

Dignified, care can often make a huge difference in your ending-of-days costs. This fact is beginning to be recognized by a growing number of health care professionals who are addressing this growing need.

Housing Choices

In your ending-of-days journey, for a variety of reasons, you may have to make choices about where to live. Many factors are involved in choosing where your ending-of-days takes place: your health costs, availability, and location to name a few.

Often the primary focus when making these choices is solely financial. However, there are also emotional costs that must be considered as making this change can be a difficult decision for both you and your loved ones. However, the key is to select the best choice from what is available. Sometimes you may want something that you cannot have. Sometimes you can find a way to have a modified version. Sometimes there is no clear way. In this situation, choose the best of what you can have.

These choices can be and are often challenging. You have the ability and the skills to choose as you have done this many times in your life. This is simply another opportunity. And, if you look ahead and have had some forethought, the decision can become easier. Also, know that sometimes the journey will require changing choices as new information and your needs change. Allow yourself to be flexible; be realistic, ask for and seek sound advice from trusted friends, family, and health care professionals.

Here is a listing of the housing options that are available.

Staying in Your Own Home

Initially, this is the preferred option for most people. It may appear to be the easiest and most comfortable for you. There are two major questions that need to be asked as you consider this option.

At What Cost?

There are costs associated with staying at home. Is your residence accessible? Are there ramps? Can you get a wheelchair down the hall to the bathroom? Is the bathroom accessible? What needs to be done to make your home accessible? Can your house accommodate you as your health declines?

What furniture needs to be moved? Does additional equipment need to be brought into the house? Do you have to buy or can you rent or borrow it? There are "lending" services available through some community organizations.

Do an honest thoughtful home assessment. You may want to ask a consultant to come in to help you with this. Many local governmental or home health agencies have staff who can help with a home assessment at no cost.

Who Will be Your Caregivers?

While family members are the "first responders," they may eventually require backup support. Is your family willing and able to provide twenty-four-hour care as your physical body weakens? What are the costs and availability of private caregiving services?

Part of staying at home is being realistic about what home care entails. Who will be the caregivers? Do they have the physical stamina and ability to give the needed care? Consider the cost of twenty-four-hour in-home care at a hypothetical fee of $25 an hour, which is probably low. You do the math as to what the daily costs can become. Ask yourself, how many hours daily do I need or can afford care? Your answer may surprise you.

Additional supplies and equipment must be added into the equation such as: incontinence supplies (adult diapers), special food supplementation, sterile supplies, and monitoring systems. These miscellaneous items can cost hundreds of dollars a month. There are other specialized equipment needs such as safety bars, special beds, and sheets. Unless insurance helps pay for in home care, it can become excessively expensive for most people.

There are advantages to remaining at home:
1. one is less agitated or confused with more peaceful familiar surroundings
2. a familiar setting helps you to remain focused and, in many cases, able to get out of the house with assistance
3. caregivers are generally family who are also comfortable in the setting

All the costs and benefits must be carefully thought out to bring the best possible care to you for your ending-of-days and for your family.

Finally, remember that inflation is driving *all* prices up. This is an essential factor with all your choices.

Independent Living Facilities

Group housing and group home options are becoming increasingly available. Many are independently organized and may or may not be licensed. Independent housing is generally the least expensive way to live, but this option usually lacks oversight by a government or health care agency. In addition, in many instances you are "living on your own." Should you need care, it is up to you to identify what is needed, arrange, and pay for the care.

There is growing interest in continuum of care communities that offer the opportunity to buy into a designated community that offers housing from independent cottages or apartments to assisted living to full skilled nursing/Dementia care and dying/hospice care. Often a wide range of amenities are offered: swimming pools, tennis courts, car service, etc.

This housing option is particularly appropriate for couples where one partner may require more care than the other. While attractive, they generally require significant "up-front" investment. When choosing this option, carefully read all details of the contract, especially if you are in a dual-need situation for both of you and this is a primary factor.

Assisted Living Facilities

Assisted living (AL) facilities are an option for many people. They are neither inexpensive , nor are they necessarily ending-of-days facilities, although people do die there. Some of these complexes require a rather large "deposit," which you may or may not get back. This policy differs markedly from one facility to another. Additionally, Medicare does not cover all costs.

In assisted living, you generally care for yourself, however, you do have a nurse on call. Most have a dining room with a range of meal options. Although rules vary from state to state, one caveat about assisted living facilities is that they require in an emergency, you must be able to get from your bed and out an exit door by yourself. If you, for example, need assistance in transferring from your bed to a wheelchair, you may not meet the requirements for living there. When you are no longer able to completely care for yourself, you are transferred to a nursing home (skilled care) or another wing within the complex if the skilled care option is available in the same facility or nearby.

Assisted living facilities can offer some assistance with your activities of daily living (ADLs) care needs. Often referred to as "care points," these add to your monthly costs. Care points can be accessed for a range of services from medication management to helping you put on your support socks. Other services like hair salon and pharmacy services are an additional cost.

Often assisted living is an attractive option in that they are readily available in most communities usually, with a number of choices. AL's often let residents bring their pets (small dogs or cats), which is always nice.

You need to review the contract and make sure you understand all costs beyond basic room and board in an AL. This includes a non-refundable damage deposit for your beloved pet. Costs vary widely between regions, size of unit, and number of services included.

Skilled Nursing Facilities /Nursing Homes

Skilled nursing facilities (SNFs) offer skilled nursing care when you are no longer able to care for yourself or when your family can no longer care for you. They also offer around-the-clock staff, call buttons for help, immediate medication for pain relief, and resources to keep you clean and comfortable. Unfortunately, nursing facilities are often full with limited space and may have a wait list for rooms. In addition, they often have high staff turnover and minimum staffing. These concerns are valid and certainly are a basis for questions to ask when you visit a facility.

Most US nursing homes are approved to accept Medicare, Medicaid, or both. The cost of nursing home care is typically higher than assisted living, and it can become very expensive. There are several factors that impact the cost of a nursing home stay, including location, length of stay, and care services required, among others.

Have you priced ending-of-days care options in your area lately? The costs of assisted and skilled care options may amaze you. Call around in your area just to get a sampling of options and costs as they vary from facility to facility Take a tour. Ask questions about staff: patient ratios, staff turnover, and facility

3 — Your Journey, Many Roads Not All of Them Are Paved

certification. Gather your data in advance so you know what you are signing up for before making your decisions.

Increasing numbers of elderly end up in skilled nursing facilities. Medicare and Medicaid programs fund a portion of facility services. Medicare long-term care services are covered by Part A, "skilled nursing facilities" (SNF) services which are associated with post-operative or post-hospitalization including rehabilitation therapies. However, when post-hospitalization coverage runs out, generally after three months or ninety days, private/personal pay kicks in.

The other coverage is by Medicaid and paid for by the state. Called "nursing facility" (NF) services, this coverage is provided to state residents who meet the Medicaid eligibility requirements. Facilities often require a period for you to be "private pay" before becoming Medicaid eligible. Additionally, Medicaid often requires a "pay-down" of resources. It is important that you understand these requirements before assuming Medicaid will pay for your care in a facility.

An eighty-eight-year-old nurse, in Florida, in her conversation with her eighty-nine-year-old husband reflects the blunt reality of ending-of-days costs. He was newly admitted to a skilled nursing facility after surgery for a critical heart condition. She was sorry to tell him, but he had ninety days of insurance to decide to recover or die since she could no longer lift him out of bed. Her husband said he understood and would think about what she had said. They didn't speak about it again. On the eighty-ninth day he died peacefully with his wife beside him. She felt a deep sense of gratitude and, in all honesty, relief.

Facility care in the US is a critical medical concern. For those with long-term care insurance to cover some of the costs, facility care may be doable. However, the experience could have staggering care costs. This should encourage you to carefully consider how realistic spending your ending-of-days in a skilled care facility really is. Be proactive—plan for and understand your options.

For those who like more specific information, Genworth Financial has compiled a list of US median long-term care services costs. While this is their most current information, remember to add inflation changes.

According to Genworth's 2020 Cost of Care Survey, (that was before rampant inflation), a private room in a nursing home costs $290 per day, or $8,821 per month. Semi-private rooms, while less expensive, average $255 per day or $7,756 per month. In some urban areas, fees may be as high as $120,000 or more a year. Like an assisted living (AL), these costs generally do not include pharmacy bills, barber or beauty shop expenses, foot care, dressings and treatments, and other miscellaneous therapies and supplies. (Used by Permission).

US Median Long Term Care Support Services Cost
Genworth Financial

Rate Type	2021 National Median Values	2020 National Median Values	One Year Increase in $$ Amount
Homemaker Hourly Rate	$26	$24	10.64%
Home Health Aid Hourly Rate	$27	$24	12.5%
Adult Day Care Services Hourly Rate	$78	$74	5.41%

Rate Type	2021 National Median Values	2020 National Median Values	One Year Increase in $$ Amount
Assisted Living Facility Monthly	$4,500	$4,300	4.65%
Nursing Home Semi-Private Room Monthly	$7,800	$7,650	1.96%
Nursing Home Private Room Monthly	$8,910	$8,700	2.4%

Source: Genworth Cost of Care Surveys 2017-2021. Conducted by CareScout® (used with permission).

Hospice

Hospice is a resource that makes both care and financial sense. There are many things to consider with hospice. While popular perception is that hospice is for imminent dying, referrals are accepted if death is expected within six months. Even this timeframe can be extended if there is declining health. You can enter hospice at any point in the dying process with an order from your physician. While there are occasional exceptions, generally hospice care is at the very ending-of-days when death is imminent, within weeks or less.

Hospice can be either at a specific location or in the home. For hospice to be in the home, there must a primary caregiver in the home, generally family or friends. The hospice nurse is like a visiting nurse and does not stay with the dying person. Rather, the hospice nurse makes frequent visits and supports the family/care givers in the ending-of-days. Check to see if hospice care is available in your community, the requirements for admission, what is included and, of course, any financial cost for you.

One of the great improvements to Medicare was the inclusion of coverage for hospice services. Added to the program in 1982, the current Medicare hospice benefit provides for a wide variety of care and services. Aside from the usual medical services, there are also provisions for home-maker services, social workers, grief counseling, and other services needed to manage your ending-of-days.

Having access to hospice, either through Medicare or other community-based programs, lets you and your loved ones navigate the many challenges of ending-of-days. Most importantly, using these programs allows you and your family to avoid unnecessary and unproductive trips to the emergency room or extended stays in the hospital. Hospice supports your decision-making and honors your ending-of-days wishes.

Hospice support allows you to access necessary care and support without the tremendous costs often associated with traditional hospital-based medical care. It provides much needed peace-of-mind for you and your loved ones on your ending-of-days journey.

It is important to clearly understand how hospice works for you and what are the program's limitations. This need is reflected in one wife's experience in Ohio. Her dying husband began to have difficulty with breathing. In a momentary panic, she called for emergency services rather than the hospice nurse. Her husband was admitted to the hospital for acute care treatment with a resultant and costly stay in the hospital. When this happens, hospice may not accept a patient back into their program as per Medicare regulations.

A Frequent Ending-of-Days Scenario

Often, it is in the last couple of weeks that care costs can spiral out of control. As you read, please consider that this is for many whose families have not planned for their last days. This is an often-repeated pattern. An emergency happens and 911 is called. From there, the person is usually admitted to an acute care hospital via the Emergency Department. Without specific pre-planning, the situation can, and often does, escalate to treating their ending-of-days as an acute condition. This is what hospitals do, this is their focus.

As a result of this redirection/redefinition of dying as an acute care condition, medical and surgical interventions are ordered. Costs can quickly increase, resulting in hundreds of thousands of dollars spent on care costs. In addition, both denial and fear of being sued may result in many hospitals attempting to "cure" the person in the final stages of life. Although this is spending money on futile care, the real consequence is the huge costs to the patient and family.

It is here, in these last weeks or days, that care expenses can exceed insurance limits and ultimately wipe out personal savings accounts. This is a sad yet often repeated scene. This makes it even more important for you to rethink how you want to receive care consistent with your ending-of-days wishes.

Should care be invasive, expensive care in a hospital or should it be in hospice at home with experienced staff who understand the nature of dying? You do have a choice to be at home with family and friends to support you. When you clearly identify what you want for you or your loved one, then you can follow your preferred choice, even during a period of crisis.

The sense of security in knowing that your care wishes will be followed during your ending-of-days allows you to relax, smile, and enjoy your remaining days. You know this feeling well as you have planned many events in your life. Since this event is the last most important event in your life, *plan it well*. Ask questions, take a tour, and gather all the data necessary for you to make this a "scenic side trip" rather than a detour full of potholes.

> *Dear family and friends,*
>
> *I know I don't write often but the past few weeks have been a time of figuring out where I want to live my ending-of-days. I have not heard that term for many years. Guess you can tell I'm getting really old. One of the counselor's used it. How's it sound to you? I feel a little scared and yet it is inevitable. It's like I'm between a rock and a hard place.*
>
> *Well, I must say I felt a little overwhelmed when I started to look at all the options I have. I really want to be at home surrounded by my loved ones. I would love that and we are working on seeing how that can happen. I didn't realize how expensive it was to die. I just thought I would close my eyes. Oh my.*
>
> *I knew that hospitals were for acute care but never had thought about being admitted at ending-of-days for an acute care condition and how many possible extra tests and procedures would or could be done. I did not understand what being admitted at this time to a hospital would mean.*

I am realizing now that I also need other things like a living will for health care. I will get started on those items as soon as I can but want to visit a couple of facilities first.

I'm still a little bit scared but I know where I'm going and feeling better about how I can end my days in comfort and peace.

All for now . . . it's time for my late afternoon walk.

Love,
M

4

Road Maps and Papers for Your Journey

Getting ready for your Last Journey can be rewarding and, in its own way, quite an adventure; you will want everything to go as smoothly as possible. As with any journey you always try to think of all the unexpected things that might occur and include some contingency plans. For instance: when you fly you may pack some snacks in your carry-on just in case the plane is delayed, or there is no food on the flight. You also include your medications and extra underwear, just in case. Take extra cash or a second credit card, just to be sure.

This is a journey of a lifetime, literally. You might have experienced another's Last journey, but this one is *your* Last Journey. You want to know what to expect so it can go with ease and flow, the way you intend, minimizing any surprises.

The road maps and papers in this chapter are designed to help ease the course as you navigate through this stage of preparation. Working with your attorney, estate planner, knowledgeable friends, and/or internet resources can assist you with greater ease and flow. Be open to ask for help and choose what fits your situation the best. It's like buying a car. You look at all that is available, the prices, the add-ons, and decide which best fits your budget and needs. Then you can create a checklist to make sure that all the details and papers needed for safe smooth travel are taken care of in advance. This planning is a gift to yourself to know that you can do these things when you are feeling well. And, if you are not feeling well, there is still time to get the paperwork completed.

Never underestimate the value of good legal documents to ease the effort of leaving this physical form, especially for your heirs. This is an important way to give you peace of mind knowing that you have attended to all the legal matters. This makes this time smoother, gentler, and peaceful, free of worry and concern for you and your loved ones.

While there are many forms that can be part of your ending-of-days journey, included in this chapter are several essential documents for healthcare decision-making.

The most important thing to remember as you create your travel documents is to make sure everything is current and easily found when needed. Like any trip, using an old road map only leads to missed directions. The same goes here.

Finally, make sure your power of attorney and executor of the estate know where everything is and can access it quickly: think keys, passwords, and combinations. Although scavenger hunts are usually fun, your attorney and executor would be much happier if that is not part of your Last Journey.

Power-of-Attorney (POA)/Attorney-in-Fact

Giving someone your power of attorney (POA) allows them to act on your behalf should you become unable to do so yourself. Your POA pays bills, does banking, helps with medical, insurance, and benefits paperwork. Without a power of attorney, when you become unable to care for yourself, a relative or interested party could begin legal proceedings to be appointed as guardian. This can be a long, tedious process and is easily avoided with a little pre-planning.

The POA is a document that needs to be witnessed and is best prepared by an attorney. It is a powerful document, so think very carefully and talk it over with the person you choose before you complete the paperwork.

When possible, it is best to name someone as an alternate POA. This person stands ready to step in if the first POA cannot serve. Both POAs need to be familiar with your stated wishes as well as your financial matters. Give them sufficient information to take care of your affairs: make decisions, pay bills, feed the pets (or arrange kennel care).

A seventy-six-year-old man from Idaho selected his wife to be his POA as she was an attorney and six years younger than him. She was reluctant to accept but since she was already taking care of his accounts, she didn't feel it was any big deal. The wife was killed in a car accident in which he was critically injured. The family was at a loss as to how to assist him and did not know where any of their bills, medical, insurance, or other papers were located. Although you might think that this wouldn't happen to you, it is critical your POA and the alternate have instructions as to where your information is kept so they can act on your behalf.

Advanced Directives

Advanced directives allow you to determine in advance your choices for your care in a crisis where you may be unconscious or otherwise unable to make/communicate a decision. Often, the advanced directive defines and guides your care wishes in your ending-of-days. Although statutes (laws) differ from state to state, advanced directives are critical for determining care. The document clearly identifies your care preferences and is binding on your family and any power of attorney. This is the document that physicians and hospital staff turn to for clear direction regarding your care and defines the scope of treatment such as resuscitation, tube feeding, and ventilator use.

Generally, your attorney prepares an advanced directive. However, many hospitals also have advanced directive forms that you can complete.

Sarah, a quirky widow living alone, fell late one night and broke her hip. She lay on the cold floor until Ann, her concerned neighbor, who didn't see Sarah letting her beloved dog out at the usual time, came to the house. Using the key Sarah had given her, Ann opened the door and found Sarah lying on the floor. Although conscious, Sarah was delirious from shock. Ann called 911; they came immediately, stabilized Sarah, and transferred her to the hospital.

At the ER, it was determined that Sarah had a broken hip and needed immediate surgery. At this point, Sarah was fully conscious and capable of her own decision-making and agreed to the surgery. However, if Sarah had been unable to make a decision, her POA, using the advanced directive and knowledge of Sarah's wishes, would have guided the decision making.

Physicians Order on Life Sustaining Treatment (POLST)

An additional form used in many states is the Physicians Order for Life-Sustaining Treatment (POLST). This document is prepared by you and your physician and states your wishes for emergency treatment. It is posted at your front door or on your refrigerator to alert emergency responders (EMTs, fire or police) as to your wishes: resuscitation or no resuscitation. It is generally printed on a brightly colored paper. Emergency workers know to look for it to give them direction. In the absence of the POLST, emergency responders will do CPR or other forms of resuscitation, which sometimes create unanticipated and undesired consequences.

Preparing a POLST with your physician is a critical step in your ending-of-days plan. Care facilities (nursing or assisted living) will require you to have a POLST as part of their admissions process.

Peter, a long-time resident of an assisted living facility, went into respiratory failure early one afternoon. EMS was called. Arriving at the facility, they found Peter's bright green POLST posted on his little refrigerator. They immediately administered oxygen and transferred him to the nearby hospital ER as per his designated wishes on the POLST.

At the ER, Peter went into full cardiac arrest. At this time, Peter's advanced directive, which was on file at the hospital, became the guiding document that allowed Peter to die peacefully with none of the drastic interventions he so feared. He managed his choices that were honored, as it should be when they are clearly identified.

Living Wills

A Living Will for Health Care Decisions is used when you become permanently unconscious or have a terminal illness. This written instrument appoints another person, in advance, to act as your health care agent if you become incapacitated. The living will provides instructions for others to make medical decisions for you when you are no longer able to make them for yourself. A healthcare agent is sometimes called a health care proxy, patient advocate, surrogate, or health care representative. This agent is usually appointed in advance to make these health care choices and decisions *only* when you are not able to make them for yourself.

By creating a living will, you may save your family the often-troubling ending-of-days decisions regarding both beginning and removing life support systems. Additionally, your planning will prevent both expense and emotional trauma

A client in Louisiana shared her repeated frustration with her large immediate family when their mother had a severe heart attack and had no advanced directives. The mother had repeatedly told her family that she didn't want any life saving measures or to be put on life support. Even so, the family was divided as what to do. As a result, because there was no living will, the mother was put on life support, never regained consciousness, and the family was left with huge hospital bills.

Today there are several ways to legally protect yourself and your loved ones through advanced directives. This is your Last Journey, and you have the right to choose how you want to end your days.

Please prepare an advanced directive and give copies to everyone in your family. Put one in your glove compartment, carry one in your purse, give one to your physician for his records. You will need this if you go to the hospital *each* time. While it should be a part of your hospital records, your previous hospital records may have been stored. It takes time for the hospital staff to retrieve them. When you enter the hospital next time, you might not have time, as it may the last time.

Take the time in advance to express your preferences for medical care, life support, and other interventions to ensure that your loved ones will not be burdened with making difficult medical decisions on their own or through the courts. Living wills may be prepared with or without an attorney. They are truly a gift of love to those who are part of your journey.

Last Will or Testament

A will is a legal document that states your last wishes; to whom to give what, and how they are to receive the proceeds. It may be completed with or without an attorney. If you avoid making a will, you may leave numerous legal problems and arguments for your survivors after your death. Making a will ensures your belongings will get to the right loved ones. Without a will, your heirs may pay extra costs, legal fees, taxes, and additional expenses. A will and last testament can also make sure other final wishes are carried out such as: funeral instructions, burial, cremation, or donations to science.

A client found her great-grandmother's will while cleaning out some of her mother's papers after her mom passed. The will was written in pencil on a torn and crumpled piece of paper. It said, "When my body is cold and gray, I want all my things to go to my daughter. Bury my body in the dirt next to my husband."

Wills can be very simple or very complex. You get to choose what you want.

Other Documents for Your Journey

Community Property Agreements

Several states have enacted Community Property Agreements as the legal standard for dealing with marital property. Very simply, a couple agrees that when one of them dies, *all* the deceased's property passes directly to the surviving spouse/partner. This agreement keeps all property/assets out of probate. However, no other heirs can be designated, only the surviving spouse.

As with any legal document, this one should be prepared by an attorney. You need to understand the implications of a Community Property Agreement.

Trusts

A trust is an effective estate-planning tool for many individuals. It is recognized as the best way to avoid probate. Probate is the legal process for distributing your property after you die. A trust is a method of holding property in a fiduciary or "trust" relationship for the benefit of the named beneficiaries or heirs. The same person may be the grantor, trustee, and beneficiary. The grantor may also name successor trustees if the original trustee dies or is unable to serve, as well as successor beneficiaries.

Many of our clients find that creating a living trust gives them peace of mind. The misinformation that many people have is that only wealthy people need or can have a trust. Even those with a modest or median income may benefit from a trust. Check it out and see if it is right for you.

To create a trust the owners of the trust (also called the grantors or settlors) make a trust document then transfer real property or other assets to the trust. Assets transferred into the trust belong to the trust and are managed by the trustee. The trustee manages the trust property for the benefit of the beneficiaries according to the terms of the trust document. There are two basic categories of trusts: revocable and irrevocable.

A mutual friend, recently divorced, decided to put her small property and assets into a revocable trust through the advice of a trusted financial planner. She was amazed with how easy it was to complete and how much she learned about her assets. As part of setting up her trust, she also did all her ending-of-days paperwork. When she finished, she gave each of her children a copy of the trust and all the ending-of-days papers plus instructed them on the importance of knowing where she keeps her trust papers, along with other important papers. She said that it gave her a strong sense of security for herself and for her family.

Trusts can provide many benefits, such as:
1. avoiding probate
2. protecting assets from creditors
3. keeping your financial affairs confidential
4. minimizing taxes, delays, and legal expenses

When your estate is distributed under a will (after you die), you lose control over what happens to it once received by your heirs. Trusts provide a way to protect and manage your estate even after your death or incapacity.

Even with small holdings, trusts can service many purposes, such as:
1. ensuring pet care according to instructions to trustees
2. protecting government benefits or Medicaid eligibility
3. maintaining financial and beneficiary choices confidentially

Revocable Trust

A revocable trust may be changed or terminated by the grantor (this is you) of the trust. The settlor (you) reserves the right to take back any trust property and remaining revenues. What this means is that although your funds and accounts are legally in the trust name, *you* (the grantor) still own and control your own money. Revocable trusts are also referred to as grantor trusts. Any assets in the trust when the grantor (you) dies become part of the grantor's taxable estate.

Irrevocable Trust

An irrevocable trust is somewhat different. The difference is that this trust can't be changed or terminated without the consent of the beneficiaries. By transferring assets into the trust, the creator of the trust (you) gives up control and ownership. Therefore, the assets and income are no longer taxable to the grantor (you), nor do they become part of the settlor's taxable estate when he or she dies. Some types of irrevocable trusts include an irrevocable life insurance trust, irrevocable family trust, Medicaid income trust, special needs trust, and charitable trusts.

There are also more complicated trusts. Examples are bypass trusts and charitable remainder trusts. In the case of all trusts, it is advisable to work with an attorney to develop any or all trust documents.

Additional Road Map Instructions

In addition to all the specific legal paperwork, it is wise to have other forms of written communication or road maps. Basically, your road map is a set of instructions that tells the executer or a responsible family member who to contact, what you would like them to do and where valuables are located. This vital bit of information clarifies details of what to do in case of an emergency or after a person's passing. It makes the job of the estate executor or the responsible person easier to handle.

Final Arrangements Preferences

This is a list of other or additional details not specified in your will or directive. For example, you might write, "Look in my wallet located in my purse in the bottom dresser drawer in the second bedroom for my medical insurance card information."

In addition, you might want to indicate how you would like your funeral to proceed and your preferences as to burial and how. For example, do you want a traditional burial or cremation? Do you have a prepaid plan if so with what funeral home? Are there certain hymns or verses you wish to be read?

Your Obituary in Your Own Words
If you are comfortable with writing a few paragraphs about what you would like others to know about your life, go ahead and write it down. You can leave a copy of this page along with a packet of all your other instructions with your survivor.

It is best if you can prepare your obituary as you know the correct names of your siblings. Make sure you include your children and grandchildren in your list of survivors. The funeral home or your local newspaper can provide an obituary template.

A note to those in second (or third) marriages; this is the case when you really need to write your own obituary or make sure you clearly state your wishes regarding how previous spouses are acknowledged. This can be tricky as there can be hard feelings.

The advice is the same for those in "partnerships" or other relationships that do not involve civil marriage. These long-term commitments need to be acknowledged.

A recent obituary of a person who lived a rather interesting and flamboyant life noted, in detail, her five marriages over her ninety years. It made for interesting reading but such detail may not be for everyone.

Data for Your Death Certificate

Write down specific information you will need for this form. This will include your date and place of birth, social security number, parents' names, education level for yourself as well as your spouse or significant other. Often, this document requires your mother's maiden (birth) name; only you may have this information.

Creating the right documents for you, properly executed, and carefully stored will give you the important tools to help you to have a graceful closure to your physical journey and assist in fostering an ending-of-days with dignity, love, compassion, and gentle release. Please look at your own documents and see what you have and what you may still need. Make a "to do" list then add a date and time as to when you are going to get each piece done.

By setting a date and time you are more likely to get things done. If you need assistance with these tasks, now is the time to ask for it. Your heirs will be so thankful you took care of these details.

You can begin to see how you can save money and time by taking care of the paperwork details now. While these tasks may seem tiresome, they are essential to assuring that your wishes are fulfilled. You and your loved ones will be so glad that you did.

Hi all,

Once I have gone through all the papers and have everything completed except my obituary—it may be time to tackle that. I never thought to write my own. And that's the interesting part. What do I really want people to know about me? I want them to remember my sense of humor and how I always looked on the bright side of things. I want people to know that my favorite color is royal blue and that I love pie and beautiful sunsets. I want people to know that I enjoyed being in nature and working in my gardens. With all my reading and life experiences, it is the little things that I think people will remember. I want people to remember how I lived and enjoyed life, not how I died. That to me will be a life well lived. I didn't mean to go on like this but sometimes it just feels good to share with all of you just how I really feel.

Trust you all are happy, well and loving your life or changing it . . .

M

5

Saying Goodbye

It's always easier to say *hello* than *goodbye*. And yet, goodbyes are meaningful because they could be the last impression that you leave with someone. There are no "do overs." Saying, goodbye is an opportunity to leave your family and friends with a treasured memory. Goodbye is a gift of closure.

When, Where, Who, to Whom and Why to Say Goodbye

Saying goodbyes may take many forms with many different people. Often distance can be a challenge. You might make a telephone call and have a long chat remembering all your good times together and how much they have meant to you over the years. Goodbyes also can be a time of saying, "I'm sorry" or, "Let's let all this go and remember the good times." Sometimes a letter or card may be in order.

For many with more advanced technology, using Skype, Zoom, or WhatsApp for face-to-face communication, or even a mobile phone with other apps, substitutes for physically being together. Technology works well to bring family into each other's personal space. That final call, whatever the approach, will be a cherished moment.

Above all, consider a good time and place to say your final goodbyes. It's true that many will remain in denial until close to the end. However, remember that this is about *you*. You get to choose the time to say your final goodbyes. Take advantage of this. Take this important time to say your goodbyes when you are relaxed and peaceful. It's never too late to be finally ready. Do it while it's on your mind.

It is important to remember in saying goodbyes to listen to what the other person is saying to you. This is a listening so deep that you feel with the other person and what they are not just saying, but rather what they are experiencing in their inner world. This is empathy. As you let go of your predetermined ideas and judgments about life and people, you discover your heart opening to this special emotion and can begin to feel the compassion, deep understanding, and love coming through. This is the most precious and endearing gift you can leave with another. You have touched them in their heart of hearts.

It is appropriate for your family to know that you are in your ending-of-days. If they are wise and loving, they will realize that knowing this is a rare and wonderful gift.

We hear you say, "How can this be?" Yes . . . rare and wonderful. Rare in that few people realize the opportunity to have this precious time to be with you moment by moment and revel in the beautiful simplicity of each moment, each task, each smile. There are now a limited number of moments, so each becomes rarer and more valued. Sharing these moments together will be treasured as precious gifts given between two grateful hearts for their time together sharing, growing, and experiencing life together.

One woman we know was dying and decided that she wanted to share a precious fun memory with all her friends. She had a large party where she showed the movie *Mama Mia*. Everyone laughed, danced, and sang loudly celebrating life—her life. Four weeks later, she died peacefully. That was 2015. To this day, when her friends think of her, they remember that party and are filled with the joy of celebrating life moment by moment that she left with them.

Who Do You Want with You at the Ending-of-Days?

Often called "gathering company," who you want with you is an important part of saying goodbye. These are the people or person you would like at your bedside in your final hour. If you have not yet thought about who you would like with you at end-of-days, now is the time. Maybe there is a friend or family member who could come and be with you as you journey through ending-of-days. As you reflect on this, decide to talk with them early to let them know you would like them to be with you at the designated time. Give them time to think about this request, then begin the conversation on how you could make this happen and what it would look like.

Linda, in Utah, asked a long-distance friend to be with her during her final days. Since they are close in heart and mind, the gentle planning grows sweeter as the years pass. They have talked about buying a plane ticket and soft sharing about her wishes. Soft sharing involves gently exploring one's wishes and meandering around them with gentle nudges to discover what she *really* wants. The conversation often goes to wishes for happiness, continued success, and being a good person. They also are beginning to talk about final gifts to family and friends such as family heirlooms, jewelry of special significance, photos, or monetary gifts prior to death.

You might not have relatives or close friends to give gifts to so you might offer some of your belongings to neighbors, service clubs or a charity. You may want to consider one or more items for your caregivers as a special remembrance. Be generous, be loving; you are leaving a memory.

Sharing Grief and Loss in Your Goodbyes

You may think that grief and loss are not things you would include in saying goodbye. Yet, each is very important at this time. Both you and your loved ones are at a crossroads of no return. It is okay for all of you to have times of sadness and tears for so many different reasons. Crying together is something that can happen naturally as an expression of deep caring. It's fine to share your feelings with the other while also saying how much you love and appreciate all the support they have given you over the years and everything you have learned and will carry with you.

Betty, in Arizona, shared a story about her father-in-law, Barry, in intensive care with few ending-of-days left. His wife, Helen, was beside herself that she could only be with him for fifteen minutes every hour. As a nurse and a minister, Betty intervened for them to have an extended time for saying goodbye. They entered the curtained cubical with all the electronic machines and Helen shuddered. Betty took her hand and walked up to the side of the bed. Barry opened his eyes staring longingly at Helen. Betty brought a chair closer so they could hold hands and Helen stroked his arms. Betty said, "You two need some time together to talk and hold each other. I'm going to stand at the curtain and make sure no one interrupts you." There were tears and low loving words exchanged.

Soon the nurse came around to see what was going on as Barry's monitors were normalizing! Betty intervened, asking again to allow them this time together. Twenty-five minutes later, Helen called to Betty to come to the bedside. The loving couple were in tears of gratitude for this precious gift of saying goodbye.

You might have family members and/or friends who have negative feelings towards you and you about them; and now, here is your ending-of-days. It appears one or both of you have no love to give nor time to spare to be together even briefly. The final question for you to ask is, "If I am to never see this person again, is this how I want to leave things?" In anger, we often make rash decisions that, in this case, cannot be physically reversed. Making peace at the ending-of-days is one of the greatest acts of forgiveness and love that anyone can offer. As you can feel, we believe in the sun even when it is not shinning.

Leaving Instructions

You have control of your final preparations *if* you speak up and take this option. The key to this is getting it done while you are healthy and before the ending-of-days has progressed. At that time, you can think clearly and can talk to as many people as necessary to get the message across. And, it doesn't have to stop with talking about your preferences. You can make the calls and select just about everything in advance. This gives you time to look at costs and make wise choices.

Last minute rushing because financial issues were not discussed beforehand often results in things costing much more in money and emotions. To achieve peace of mind, you need to think about what you would like, what others have done, and what suits you. In short, this is your final farewell, and you can do it your way. This is *your* ending-of-days. Make it what you want and smile.

Looking Your Best

Probably the last thing you think about when making your leaving instructions is what to wear to look your best. Yet, this is important because you will not have a mirror to look into before the big event. The fact remains that you want to look your best. How many times have you gone to a viewing and said or heard someone say, "Oh, she doesn't look like herself." You need to have photos available in which you do look your best— your hair, your coloring, and your makeup or lack thereof. These photos need to be known and accessible to your family or loved ones so there is no last-minute scramble to find the right picture.

If you are choosing cremation or closed casket, you do not have this option as your last viewing is usually at bedside while there is still some slight color in your cheeks and you are still warm. For a growing number of people cremation is becoming their choice. They want to be remembered for who they were and how they loved others rather than what they looked like.

Choosing Your Travel Outfit

Clothes you look good in and what others think you look good in can be very different. We all have been in stores where the salesclerk has said how great we look in something. When we get home and try it on, it just doesn't look all that great. The same is true when choosing your final travel outfit. Choose something that you like that has colors that you usually wear. This is *not* the time for that far-out suit or outfit that only you

5 — Saying Goodbye

liked or it is a color that you usually don't wear. This is the time to select what looks great on you. Remember that usually only your upper half is seen, so shoes and socks are not necessary. Do not feel obliged to buy something new! This journey does not require a new wardrobe.

Along with selecting your outfit comes the question of jewelry. The same advice goes here: decide to wear what you like. Often a wedding ring or favorite ring is on the hand. Be sure to let your family and the funeral home know that you want your jewelry removed and returned to the family after the viewing and before the burial.

Some religious traditions have a custom of being buried with a religious object: crucifix, rosary, Star of David, or other items. Please let your family know if this is your preference and where the items are located. They will be so thankful that you did.

Make a list of everything that you want to wear and where it is located. *And* let your family know where both the list and the desired items are located. Once again, they will be grateful that you did.

Finally, this is *not* the time to try a new hairdo. Many funeral facilities have their own hair stylist. However, in smaller communities, often your personal hair stylist can prepare you for viewing. Having a picture available of a "best hair look" is helpful.

One of our friends is a "clothes horse" and always perfectly put together. Her greatest ending-of-days fear was leaving clothing choices to her husband, who neither knew nor cared about style and fashion. She entrusted three close women friends with her explicit instructions as to what she was to wear for her cremation.

Yes, cremation. She believed in looking good to the very end, even if that end was an urn of cremains. Of course, she preselected the perfect urn to reflect her life-long sense of taste and style. Going in style can be your choice.

Final Resting Preparations
Planning can create peace of mind not only for you but also your loved ones after you are gone. Planning now is a selfless act and a last gift to your loved ones that extends beyond your end-of-days.

Prepared/Prefunded Arrangements
Prepared arrangements, often called pre-planning, is becoming increasingly popular. This means you select the funeral home and make the arrangements ahead of time. Your family will truly value this forethought. There are three types of preplanning.

1. **Wishes Identified**: arrangements are on file with the funeral home, a family member, or the executor for your estate and preferably all three. These are *not* prepaid.
2. **Insurance Funded Policies:** This policy is with a preselected funeral home and locks in the price. It is sometime transferable if you move out of the area, however, be sure to check this with the agency before you purchase the policy. An insurance funded policy is the easiest for your family at the time of death. Policy payments may be made on a monthly basis or in a lump-sum and may be purchased at any time. Funeral policies

are highly regulated, so check with your local funeral home to understand these requirements.
3. **A Funeral Trust:** This is a policy purchased from a funeral home that then places the money in trust at a bank. The money cannot be used until the time of death. These policies work like a savings account that you can access for only *one* item, a funeral. However, the trust may not cover all costs. Nonetheless, they are an appropriate choice for many people. Presently these are more difficult to get since the money in the trust is not making much interest to help cover the increasing costs over time.

There are major benefits to prepared/prefunded final arrangements. Often, most if not all, of the financial resources have been used up with nursing homes, in-home care or simply living longer. As a result, there may be little—if any—money to pay for the final arrangements. Remember that the funeral costs must be paid in full before both the funeral and the disposition (how the body is prepared). There may be an occasional exception, but those are rare.

Within families there are also benefits to prefunding besides costs. Adult children don't always get along. At this time, they can get highly emotional with different opinions on what to do regarding costs, especially if they have to help pay for your funeral. The bitterness and hurt generated from this conflict can last a long time. Therefore, your preplanning helps to diminish and often eliminate some of this emotional and financial discomfort.

Your prepared/prefunded funeral is akin to a celebration of your life, which adds to gentle closure by:

- relieving your family from stressful decisions
- assuring your personal wishes
- shelters funds if admitted to a nursing home
- guarantees inflation-proof funeral plans
- gives you and your family peace of mind
- allows you to select cremation, funeral plans, monuments, etc.
- provides arrangements according to your wants and needs

Do You Want to Plan Your Own Funeral?

Think of this as planning a very important event in your life, which it is. The other most important event in your life was your birth, where you had no input. Now *this* is your moment, your last moment, and you can plan how you want it to be. Most people really don't like to think about their mortality, much less plan for it. Planning your own funeral means realizing you are mortal and will one day die. It also means preparing for the inevitable, your ending-of-days. So why plan now? For this very reason, no one knows when they will die. However, the likelihood grows greater the longer you live.

There are ten areas of planning for your funeral. Let's explore each one so you have a direction to move in and the basic information to get started.

1. What type of funeral?

There are seven types of common funerals. Surprised? You are probably aware of a couple of them that are most common where you live. The funeral types are based on how the body is prepared, which is called a disposition.

Traditional Burial
This is the most familiar type of burial where the body is embalmed and casketed for burial in a cemetery.

Cremation
This is the second most common burial type where most of the body is literally "turned into light" by fire with some ash and bone fragments left. The cremains (ashes) are placed in an urn. During recent years, this has become the most frequently selected funeral type.

Green Funeral
This funeral is about the chemical free preparation of the body which is casketed in either a cloth shroud or a biodegradable casket. This allows the body to naturally decompose.

Green Funeral and Green Burial
This funeral incorporates the green funeral described above coupled with burial in a green cemetery in which no insecticides and pesticides are used.

Home Funeral
In this instance the family and friends lovingly wash and dress the body then place ice or dry ice beneath the deceased. In this way, the body is preserved for about three days in which time the burial or cremation can take place.

Burial at Sea
This is both a funeral and an internment. The body is wrapped in cloth or casketed, then is released into the sea during a funeral service.

Cryonic Preservation
This is the practice of preserving the body of the deceased who is legally dead through freezing. It is considered quite controversial and has limited use.

2. Who needs to be notified?

- family
- spouse/ex-spouse(s)
- children/grandchildren
- parents
- grandparents
- siblings
- other relatives
- friends
- neighbors and former neighbors
- work colleagues
- professionals who have worked for /with you
- spiritual leader: clergy, rabbi, priest, Imam
- employer
- insurance agent
- lawyer
- accountant
- doctors
- banker/financial advisor
- creditors

- organizations
- Social Security Administration
- religious: church, temple, mosque
- employers: current or former
- military service contact Veterans Administration
- places where one volunteers
- clubs: hobbies, book, sport
- alumnae organizations: high school, college
- fraternal organizations
- charities of your choice
- political organizations

3. Styles of Funerals

Today, the actual funeral may also be called a gathering or celebration of life. There are many funeral styles to choose from: traditional/formal services to destination funerals. They can be combined in any way you desire. Select what you are most comfortable with.

A Living Funeral
This gathering is centered on someone who is in active ending of days. Also known as ending-of-days or goodbye parties, they celebrate and honor the life that is still being lived. Often, bon voyage or moving away cards are given with many well wishes.

Traditional Funeral Service
This is a formal service with music, reading, a eulogy and/or inspirational message to pay tribute to the one who has passed and to give solace to those remaining behind. It usually occurs

within days of the death and prior to the burial. The location is either a place of worship or the funeral home.

Visitation or Viewing
This is a time for the family and friends to gather with the casket open for a final acknowledgement and farewell.

Home Funeral
This is a funeral held at a home, usually a relative's. The friends and family act as the funeral director to wash and dress the body. Ice or dry ice is placed beneath the deceased (out of view). The body lies in a bed or casket. The body can be kept this way for about three days. A home funeral allows family and friends an extended time for gathering, viewing, ceremonies/rituals, and fellowship.

Committal, Internment, or Graveside Service
This service occurs at the place where the body/cremains will be buried or placed. This service is an extension of the service begun at the church/temple/funeral home. A committal or graveside service may also be the only service.

Interment Service
This service accompanies the placement of the ashes into a permanent memorial site such as a mausoleum, a niche in a wall, columbarium, memorial garden, memorial ocean reef, or other permanent site.

Memorial Service
A memorial service occurs without the presence of the body and may be held weeks or even months after the death. It is often

used to allow people from great distances time to travel and arrive to be part of the service. Cremains may be present.

Scattering Service
A Scattering Service entails the actual scattering of the cremains usually in a selected location that is meaningful to the deceased.

Reception
The reception, also known as a wake, is a gathering of friends and family. It may take place at the visitation, before or after the service. It usually involves food often brought in by your family and friends or it can be a catered event or a meal in a restaurant. The choice is yours and you can plan it and prepay it!

Family/Friends Gatherings
These are generally less formal events where people related (kin or friendship) to each other gather to honor/celebrate the deceased. Some families observe the anniversary of the loved one's passing. Others may observe the anniversary of the rebirth into spirit as part of their beliefs in the hereafter. Irrespective of reason, it remains a time to celebrate the life of the deceased.

Destination Funeral
This service involves a group of family and friends who travel to a place of special meaning for an intimate memorial service.

Direct Burial
This involves cremation or burial without any viewing or service.

4. Setting the Funeral Tone

After selecting the style of your funeral, it is also important to select the tone for your funeral. This gives the organizers a definite guide to ensuring your last wishes.
    What would you like:
- solemn and reverent
- peaceful and reflective
- joyful remembering
- getting it to flow naturally
- focus on an idea (be specific: positive memories, funny experiences, etc.)
- does not make any difference

5. Service and Reception Checklist

The thing about planning is that you control the event and the costs. If you do not care, you do not have to choose. You can trust your loved ones to make an excellent selection. After all, this is really all about them and helping them to feel better and to have one last memory.

Who is in charge?
Choose a family member or loved one to work with the funeral director or church director so that the service runs smoothly. There are also funeral planning concierges and service event planners to assist in this process. However, if you are comfortable with all the decision-making then proceed on your own. Having prepaid and preplanned arrangements is often helpful for your family.

Where is the service or reception to be held?
- funeral home
- place of worship: church, temple, mosque
- outdoors: backyard/park/beach/mountains
- reception site: home, restaurant, rented site, community center
- special significance location: theater, swimming pool, beach, library, golf course

Who will officiate?
- loved one or friend
- clergy
- celebrant: someone legally authorized to conduct the service

Is there a tribute display?
This is a collection of photos from your life and special objects of meaning. With photos you might want to include date and location.

Do you want flowers?
People often request no flowers but rather donations to a special charity. Many ask that they receive flowers while they are alive so they can enjoy their scent and beauty and all the love surrounding them.
- easel display of wreath (everlasting life), heart or cross
- flower spray on top of casket
- flowers for grave side
- flowers for around the urn
- flowers for special people in your life

- plants or seasonal bulbs growing in pot for loved ones

Is there to be music and/or special songs?
- make a list of your favorite songs to be sung
- attendees or soloist to sing particular songs, hymns
- recorded music
- live music, jazz band, bagpipes, mandolin, string quartet, organ

Are there to be readings?
- scriptures, poems, essays
- Who will read them?

Do you want a eulogy?
A eulogy is a talk in honor of the deceased.

Are there any specific things to include or exclude in the eulogy?
- Who would you like to deliver the eulogy?

6. Are you a veteran and want to receive veteran's death benefits?

Veterans are eligible to receive burial at a national cemetery, a funeral flag, grave marker, and other benefits. You will need to document your military service to receive these benefits. Generally, presenting your DD-214 is sufficient:
- do you want to be buried in a national cemetery?
- do you want your family to receive a funeral flag?

- do you want the us flag displayed at your funeral?
- folded on top of the casket?
- who do you want to keep the US flag?
- do you want a grave marker?

Do you want a hearse at your funeral?
A hearse is a commonly used vehicle to transport the casket or urn to the interment site.

There are several different types of transport.
- traditional
- motorcycle procession
- horse drawn

7. Burial Details: What are your preferences?

- casket/vault
- viewing
- pallbearers
- burial site service
- burial marker/inscription and what will it be made of?
- purchase grave liner

8. Cremation Details: What are your preferences?

- view body before
- keep remains to give to someone for later internment or scattering
- store in urn

- place in cemetery or columbarium niche
- remains divided and given to different people
- disperse remains in specific manner

9. Your Obituary

- Do you want one?
- What would you like it to say?
- Who do you want named as survivors? This can be an issue in many families.
- Would you like memorial donations? If yes, name the designated charities or groups.

10. Other Arrangements and Last Words

- body/organ donor
- prepaid funeral package with funeral home/funeral concierge service
- purchased cemetery plot
- sample of DNA collected: Some states require DNA sample; the family must pay for this.
- like DNA collected before final disposition of body
- final thoughts on my funeral and in general

Considering Relatives

Ah yes, *relatives*. They come in many shapes, sizes, opinions, and life experiences. With the actual ending-of-days,

5 — Saying Goodbye

the physical and spiritual worlds become very close. The veil between the two worlds becomes thin. To your relatives and friends, this may become a reminder of their own mortality rising to the unspoken surface with many different thoughts and emotions emerging. Please know that each one will handle grief in their own way. Many cultures have special rituals to assist in this process and families are often closer during this time.

The legacy that you leave can be a great inspiration and comfort to your family and friends. For those left behind, this is a time of remembering and allowing the sting of loss to gradually be replaced with cherished memories . . . memories of how you lived rather than how you ended your days.

> *Dear loved ones,*
>
> *I cannot believe all the things there are to do and think about in saying goodbye. I am glad that I can look at all these things now while I am still healthy. And I just realized that even if I am not feeling well, I can still work on these things a little bit at a time. And I can always ask for help. I like thinking about what is best for me and for my family. I have always been the one to plan the vacations and the big events. This is another big event. Funny, I always felt like I needed to know all the answers. Now I get to ask the questions. I've made a list of what I want to get done. Don't be surprised if I call you for help.*
>
> *This is a great journey for me. Maybe when the time comes you can take the Last Journey like this too.*
>
> *Kisses and hugs,*
> *M*

6

You Have Options

Let's face it, we are all going to die. Intellectually you know this. It's the emotional part that scares us. In general, you have learned to deal with frightening emotions. Yet, consciously or unconsciously, most of us are in denial as to any fear around death. To be able to say or even to admit to yourself that, "I'm afraid," is a huge step forward.

Denial and other defense mechanisms are used all the time to protect us from real and perceived threats. Unfortunately, denying attention to something doesn't stop things from happening. At one time or another, in one way or another, all of us will die. How this fact is accepted makes preparation for death very different.

You have choices. You always have a choice. You can go out with grace and dignity or—in the worst-case scenario—kicking and screaming, leaving chaos in your wake. How do you want to go?

Waking up and accepting this emotional fact that we are all headed elsewhere, makes the future much more palatable. This place we are headed is known as many things and in many ways. Some call this destination the mysterious hereafter,

Heaven, the afterlife, being with God, Nirvana, the Great Mystery, or the great Unknown.

So, stop and ask yourself, will I die one day? And, as you answer yes, how do you plan to deal with this fact?

Are We Consciousness or Solely a Physical Being?

At the heart of the issue of dying, perhaps the primary question to ask is: are you a person of consciousness or solely a physical being? This is not a simple question. It has been debated and discussed by philosophers and scholars for millennia. The current trend in thinking, which we support through lived experience is, you are consciousness in a physical body. There are times you are physical and use your physical brain to figure things out; there are other times you are consciousness and have access to all the universal knowledge.

Knowing this, who wouldn't want to have all that knowledge? Everyone has experienced that there is something more than our physical body: when in nature, watching a sunset, a sunrise or having our breath taken away with exquisite music, a delightful taste, or beautiful words. Finding the balance between physical being and consciousness assists you to successfully navigate on this planet *and* to make choices that are in your best interest rather than out of fear or pressure from our well-meaning loved ones.

Graceful Aging All Along the Way

Research on healthier lifestyles suggests that more years can be added to your life span. It is never too late to start a healthier lifestyle, though results may vary. One thing is for sure: to gracefully move through your days is life enhancing and results in a positive attitude and often a zest for living. A sense of humor greatly aids your aging process. The ability to laugh at yourself is healthy, as your body responds by releasing endorphins. These "feel good" hormones raise your mood and relax your body. It's like wearing life like a loose set of clothes and taking yourself lightly. As you laugh others around you will laugh also and their bodies will also respond releasing endorphins. In fact, the very act of smiling sends a message to the brain that things are okay and endorphins are released. So, smile more—great big smiles that show your teeth and make your eyes twinkle.

One wise client in her eighties said, "I have a choice to laugh or cry. I choose to laugh because when I do, I always can find something humorous about what is happening . . . even when I broke my leg."

Whatever your age, live gracefully. Accept the aging process and change the things that can be changed. It is also good to know the difference between what one must accept and what one can modify. Graceful aging is greatly enhanced through gratitude. It's being able to let go of what we were able to do or accomplish in the past and be thankful for what we are able to accomplish today. It is to be able to smile when we are tired and allow our body the time to rest and replenish. It is being able to ask for help in a kind loving way and in turn, to accept help in a kind loving way. It is knowing that many things do not need to be done immediately and can wait. It is being okay where we are, who we are and what we are.

Graceful aging allows life to move at its own pace rather than pushing and pulling to get the last ounce out of the day or our body. Graceful aging is enjoying our children, our grandchildren, our friends, and ourselves at whatever age we or they are.

We all have been young; we all will grow old. Wherever we find ourselves is just the perfect place to be and rejoice because that is where we are. To paraphrase Mae West, the goddess of vaudeville, "Oh, baby, it's not the years in your life; it's the life in your years."

Experiencing Grief and Loss

While grief and loss are usually associated with the actual ending-of-days, these emotions and challenges often begin with a diagnosis. These feelings happen for the one facing dying as well as for their loved ones. Grief and loss happen on a regular basis throughout your life, yet here we are looking at the ending-of-days. Whether directly or indirectly, grief is a part of the process. Usually the closer the relationship, the stronger the grief response. In turn, grief affects every part of your life...health, emotions, relationships, spirituality, meaning of life, and even taking care of yourself.

With increasing physician visits, there are usually more tests and therapies that may become the focus of your life. As the news of deteriorating health continues, visits from family and friends increase and are welcome. However, at the same time, there is a gradual and natural withdrawing from your outer activities as your Last Journey becomes more reflective and inner focused.

You will find that your thoughts and activities slowly become increasingly focused on the immediate and short term. You may even discover that you are redefining you hopes and dreams. At this time, relief from pain may become more important than recovery. The present moment becomes where you want to live and enjoy what is happening or oftentimes, just getting through the day. Any pleasure of being present has a calming effect on you and others. Often, you may find yourself being of comfort and inspiration to your family and friends.

For most people, there is a place of internal quietness that many associate with their spiritual practices. It serves as a place of refuge and safety, which becomes of greater importance as you begin to move into a place of acceptance of your ending-of-days. As the veil between the physical and spiritual world thins at the ending-of-days, this place of inner quiet becomes a comfort and assurance even if you have not had a "spiritual/aware" life. This inner quiet place invites you to increasingly be in the present moment and in a place of "allowing" as your body continues its process of gently closing.

This is a place that we all can reach when we realize that we cannot change what is happening. When death appears inevitable, the way we die becomes important. Yes, this is the place where you still have a choice. You can choose to accept this normal, natural process of the body closing and move into a place of grace and tenderness that assists a gentler release *or* go kicking and resisting. You always have a choice; choose wisely.

Grief and Relief

Grief and relief are like the Chinese Yin Yang symbol of opposites. Other examples are positive and negative, hot and cold, sweet and sour, high and low. These opposites can be likened to a double-edged sword as they are applied to anticipatory grief and relief. Anticipatory grief is both before and after the ending-of-days as is what we may call the phenomena of anticipatory relief. You or your loved ones may have one, none, or both of these often powerful responses. So, to be prepared, let's briefly look at both.

Anticipatory Grief—The Parallel Journey

Anticipatory Grief is a deeply personal and painful journey for two people. It is a parallel journey in that while sharing the same physical space, it is a journey to two entirely separate and distinct destinations—Death and Life.

For the dying person, the ending is "known" but for the loving caregiver, the end is unknown. Dealing with the unknown is challenging in so many ways. It is often compounded by many emotions and emotional swings including anger, fatigue, guilt, and fear for both the present and the future.

With the day-to-day of decision-making and survival, the caregiver is always thinking, "What is next?" The ongoing grief is partnered with fears, both real and imaginary: loss of income, medical bills, loss of home, and the loss of the loved one.

There is also the awareness of a new loneliness, even before you are alone. The loneliness of medical decision making varies for each of us but can be very difficult for some. While you, as the primary caregiver, can seek advice from many sources, ultimately the final decision is yours alone. There may be sleepless nights dealing with medications and care giving, outbursts from your loved one, and unexpected worries running through your mind as the journey to death continues. For many, nighttime anxiety becomes the common bond during this journey.

Often the silent cry is, "Will this never end? How do I survive?" And in the silence, you know that you have to keep on going. You will and you must!

At some point the parallel journey ends; your beloved fellow traveler is gone, and your journey continues in a new direction, and it is a solo journey. You have survived.

Antidote for Anticipatory Grief

In truth, there is an antidote for anticipatory grief. This time of "watchful waiting" is an opportunity to become more aware of where you are in your life process. This is the time to realize that life can only be lived in the present moment. Just as we can only laugh in the present moment, it is discovering the little things that can give you great joy. . . the beauty of a sunset, the laughter of a grandchild, the smell of roses. It is a quick cup of coffee shared with a trusted friend Your life is about each moment and not waiting until something happens; rather it is enjoying the steps and sights along the way.

Since you don't know your end point and *no one* knows; and you don't know all the twists and turns along the way and *no one* knows; and you cannot know everything, *no one does*. Then, why waste your time in dread or fear? Rather *carpe diem*, which is the Latin phrase for "seize the day." Live each day to the fullest. Have fun and endeavor to find the fun in all you do.

It may sound odd, but another way of understanding the journey lies in the Serenity Prayer. You may already know it, but here is a reminder:

God grant me the serenity to change the things I can change;
Accept the things I cannot change and
the wisdom to know the difference.

Acceptance is the key to being happy. When one realizes that there are some things that you and I cannot change, then we can stop resisting, stop wasting our lives, and focus our attention on what we can change. You cannot change the fact that you are growing older. You cannot change the fact that you missed your dental appointment. There are many things that you cannot change. Your strength comes from seeing what cannot be changed and moving to another solution or merely laughing.

A friend in Vermont laughingly said that her mother would say, "Marvelous" and softly laugh. It would change the whole atmosphere and whatever happened suddenly would not be upsetting. They could begin looking for the solution.

As another friend's mother was declining in health, she needed to rest in the afternoon. For her, rest meant lying down in bed, which she did willingly. Often, she would want to "lazy talk," which is a combination of talking and resting often with longer pauses between sentences or thoughts and even a little dozing. One afternoon she asked her daughter to lie down with her and lazy talk. The daughter needed to go to the grocery store that afternoon, but she didn't have a grocery list nor had she looked at the ads. She thought a moment, smiled, and replied, "Just a minute." She left the room and returned with a pencil, paper, and the grocery ads. Lying down with her mother, the daughter put her arms up and opened the paper so they both could see the ads.

Her mother laughed and said, "You're so smart." It's these small things that make for great memories of everyday life.

What we are working with in our life—in both the big and small things—is basic physics; a body in motion tends to stay in motion until acted upon by an outside force. *And* a body at rest tends to stay at rest until acted upon by an outside force. Let's be proactive, get in motion and stay in motion, taking action and getting things done! In fact, in this lifetime, physics works all the time for and against us. Let's keep it working for us and keep moving mentally, emotionally, and physically so we can stay in balance and live a life with greater ease and flow.

This is the time for cherishing everyday life because you don't know, no one knows, when or what will happen next. A great part of this living more in the present moment is starting to delegate and identify when you need help. Ask for help and more importantly, accept help. In those times when you start to feel frustrated, tired, or angry—*stop*, take some deep breaths, and change what you are doing. Get up, move around, go outside, hug a tree, take a walk, put on some uplifting music, laugh, watch a funny movie, and say, "Marvelous."

A friend with terminal cancer put up signs in her home instructing her friends that she only wanted happy, uplifting visits with laughter and hugs. If they couldn't do that, then don't come around. She had no time for anything in her life but celebrations and laughter. As a result, she received huge doses of cheer and positivity resulting in good natural body secretions of endorphins and thus, whether it was scientific or not, her pain was minimal.

Some leading scientists hypothesize that negative feelings will pass quickly if you become conscious and recognize when this is happening and don't let them stop your forward momentum. This is a component of the mind-body connection. Another tenant is that a body at rest will stay at rest until acted upon by an outside force, and that is *you*. Translate this to getting out of your chair and get moving!

And, of course, if you are facing end-of-days yourself, it is critical that you take care of yourself: get enough sleep, stay on a good eating plan, be with people or talk to friends every day, stay warm and drink, drink, drink enough water to stay hydrated. Then as you can, do the same for your significant other and/or those around you.

This can become a significant time to rethink what is important. It is not so much what we should not do but what we can do to add a bit of pleasure to every one of our precious days. How much and how many limitations should we self-impose as we approach the end-of-days?

Ben and Mary were college sweethearts, married for nearly fifty years. Ben, an independent thinker who marched to his own drum for eighty years, developed a serious heart condition. Mary, his wife, assumed the role of caregiver.

Upon discharge from the hospital, while knowing his heart condition was terminal, his very youthful care team advised Ben that he must go on a salt-free diet and delete many of his favorite foods from his menu. Mary, taking the medical team's directions very seriously, busied herself revising meal plans as well as hiding all the saltshakers.

Ben tried his best to comply with the new "salt rules," but very shortly his old cravings returned. Bags of potato chips showed up for his midnight snacks or when Mary was out of the house. Ben craved salt. He tried to hide the evidence, but as time passed, he did not care. Potato chips and other "forbidden foods" became part of his daily intake.

Mary's reaction was slow at first, but she quickly became what we may term, the "salt police." She didn't intend to do or have anything bad happen to Ben, and was unconscious about her patrolling and enforcement behavior. Ben became the salt offender and Mary, the dominant person, became the "police patrol."

It wasn't until Ben died that Mary looked back and understood what had happened. Her best intentions to keep Ben safe and aid in his recovery hadn't worked. He was dying and salt restrictions were not going to change this fact. She felt badly that she policed her loved one to the end. Despite all of Mary's best, well-intentioned efforts, Ben died—still loving his potato chips.

There is an end to mortal life. Live your last days with no regrets and metaphorically, without becoming the "salt police." Let the last days be less controlled. Eat what you enjoy, or let your significant other do the same. Enjoy: ice cream, bacon, and—yes—the potato chips. Alter the rules when you are dying. Be happy.

This is a journey of a lifetime, literally. You might have experienced another's Last Journey, but this one is *your* Last Journey. You want to know what to expect so it can go with ease and flow, the way you intend, minimizing any surprises.

These simple things will help you in every way to stay in the present moment and celebrating your life. Why celebrate? Because celebration is all about you and your unique journey.

What if you could live your life, every part of it, celebrating the wins and learning from the mistakes? This is *huge*. It might be a brand-new way of looking at your life. You can do this. We have seen many, many people who are living examples of making each day their best day yet. Sometimes a simple truth comes from an unexpected source. This is the case with the cartoon character SpongeBob SquarePants, as he prophetically exclaims, "Today is the best day yet! Today is the best day yet! Today is the best day yet *because* . . ." Perhaps the creators of SpongeBob were actually helping children to keep an open, positive perspective. And this is what you need to try too.

Anticipatory Relief—The Journey Ends and Begins

At some point with your death, your survivor generally comes to a sense of overwhelming relief. It sounds strange, but true; with the ending comes the new beginning for the loved one who remains. The old journey ends and a new one begins, complete with memories of the old.

For the survivor who has spent hours, days and, perhaps, years experiencing stress, fatigue, sleep deprivation, and a constant sense of being overwhelmed, the relief death brings can be shocking. Initially, the sense of relief may leave the survivor with a feeling they may be unable to acknowledge much less talk about.

But relief it is. A weight has been lifted. The loved one has died. Relief and, yes, possibly joy comes from knowing that the pain and suffering for both of you is over. You, the survivor, is relieved: there is no one to fix meals for, no medication schedules, no interrupted sleep. The loved one is at peace and the survivor is relieved.

The parallel journey has ended and there remains but one on what was a journey for two. Thus, the caregiver, no longer a care giver, begins alone and begins anew.

Many people report, often in a lowered voice, that they still feel the presence of their loved one, especially at night in bed. They also report that they imagine them hovering above them gently moving into the cosmos. The pain of the absence is very real. The sensation slowly begins to fade as one becomes comfortable with being alone. The relief gently shifts to memories full of love and joy.

Relief is good; it is a normal, natural part of the ending-of-days. A new journey, one that is "alone but not lonely," begins for the survivor.

Lost? Ask the Right Questions

There are three *important* questions you need to ask yourself now and each day as your health and care needs change as you or your loved one enter this Last Journey. These questions lay the foundation for your care and are a guide for your decision making.

First Question

Do you want to surround yourself with the latest and greatest technology to prolong life with scant regard for the pain, suffering, comfort, or happiness involved *or* do you want the best care and decision making that decreases your suffering and gives you a gentler ending of days? You cannot have it both ways.

Second Question

Today, the closing phase of ending-of-days often looks something like this. There is an increasing series of emergencies for which medical care can only give fleeting and brief, then briefer relief. Dr. Qawande, in his book *Being Mortal*, calls this the ODTAA Syndrome, meaning: one damn thing after another. The situation is that this ending-of-days road is often unpredictable. The pauses between emergencies are variable sometimes with little rest between or other times lengthy pauses. Unfortunately—or fortunately—after a certain point, the direction of this route becomes clear. The question then becomes, for what *purpose*?

Consider what many others at this point in their life are beginning to accept. Take what time you have and realize that the finality of what time is left is actually a gift. It is a precious gift for you to redefine your life's identity into something new. And this gift is genuine independence and freedom! You might not be able to control your circumstances, but you are becoming the author of what your life means and are in control of what you do with your life.

Third Question

The last question is possibly the most important as it brings the reality of ending of days into clearer focus, "How can you make this day and every day a good day? What are the best decisions that you can make *based on your available choices*?"

When you make the best decision, the one that is the most supportive of you and what you want, that is a very good day. After making those decisions then you can plan how you can move through those hours. When you know you have made a good decision, your whole body relaxes, you smile and nod your head. Your body responds with endorphins, those feel good hormones secrete into your blood stream as if to say, thanks, here's your reward, you chose well.

During time together, one friend, through tears, sang to her friend a song a mutual friend had composed for her birthday. The words were haunting, yet revealed the depth of love expressed to her. "Today would be a good day to live or die. Today would be a good day to live or die. For today the sun is shining and tonight the moon will rise. Today would be a good day to live or die." And then the friend replied, "I love you dearly."

Today is a very good day for you, too. For today, that wonderful, exciting, one-of-a-kind *you* has the opportunity to look at options and make the choices that are the very best fit for you. Be kind and loving to yourself, and make your decisions about what is best for *you*. This is your journey and you get to choose for your best interests. When others take their Last Journey, they get to choose what is best for them.

That is how it is supposed to work.

Blessings on your journey!

Hi there,

I have been really busy looking at all the choices that I have and they are many and *I get to choose. I'm going to start being bolder. Yes, that's my new word,* bolder. *And, I'm going to start saying . . .* marvelous. *I never realized how many choices that I have. I finally realized that it's me that makes it a very good day. I'm* grateful *for today,* period. *I hope you folks are well and maybe you can help me stay bold and grateful.*

See you soon,
M

7

Arriving at Your Destination

You are almost at your destination. You have been a receptive traveler going gently into areas that you needed to know about, sending notes home to family and friends and even having some laughs and celebrating along the way. In many ways, you have been discovering that "knowing" takes a lot of the fear out of your ending-of-days. When you know what to expect, you feel more prepared and can see where you are. The best thing is now you have this road map, which can be very helpful in making sure you are as prepared as you can be.

Your Ending-of-Days Process

The ending-of-days process is a personal journey that usually begins well before the physical death of the body. No one knows for sure the date and time of their death. As you age, your body slowing down becomes more noticeable. There is a tendency to progressively think increasingly about ending-of-days. Your body taking longer to heal from minor cuts or bruises is one example of the beginning of this process. Most of us do not share these thoughts with each other or our family. When disease is part of the ending of day's process, consciously or unconsciously, most people consider their impending death and have some manner of preparation, including watchful waiting. Even not preparing is a preparation.

The Day Before You Die and Why Doing What Really Matters Is Important

What would you do differently if you knew that tomorrow you were going to die? Pay attention to how your mind responds to this question . . . What would you do: eat red raspberry ice cream, watch the sun set, tell your family how much you love them, take a long walk in the park, smell flowers, make a gratitude list, wash your hair . . . What would you do?

And here is the secret to a happy life . . . Why wait to begin these important little pleasures? No one knows when they going to die. Everyone thinks it is far away even when they are dying.

So do the things each day that bring you great joy and love; it's never too late so start now.

Here is a recently shared story. Early one evening, a friend was deep into a project when her oldest adult daughter called and asked if she could come over, perhaps bring some freshly cut flowers, and hang out for a while. The mother said, "Yes, come over, how delightful." While the daughter was driving over, the friend had an intuitive nudge to turn on the TV and see what movie they might watch. Just as her daughter was coming in the door, the mother saw that a happy, old movie was coming on next. Her heart opened and as they hugged, she asked if her daughter might like to see it. Her daughter's response was a great smile of delight. As they snuggled down to enjoy the film, she put her arm around her daughter, and for a time they were lost in a story of gentle love, magical creations, and the coming together of a silent deep love and appreciation for each other.

If our friend were to die that night, she said that she spent her last evening perfectly. What you do now really matters.

The Big "D" Itself

When you arrive at this important place, your priority is to step back and allow your body to take over more and more. It knows exactly what needs to be done. As many women know, it's sort of like having a baby. As the labor pains become regular and keep increasing in strength, you realize that you have no control over them. Then you have two choices: either fight and resist as the contractions hurt more, or breathe and allow your body to do the work. That is the key. This is the time you stop trying to be in control but instead to breathe and allow your body to do what it knows exactly how to do. This is a very big part of "letting go" and means that when you relax and focus on your breath the process is much gentler.

It's sad, in a strange sort of way, that something, which happens to everyone, is one of the things we know the least about. When we were an agricultural society, people knew about the life cycle and observed it so frequently it was commonplace. With several generations living under the same roof, someone was either coming (being born) or going (dying). As we became industrialized, many people moved to the city and we lost experiencing this natural cycle of life.

The good news—and we are repeating it again because it is so important—your body is specially designed so its systems close down through a sequential slowing down, and eventually stop with the heart's last beat.

What you want to remember is that this closing down is a normal, natural process. Once you better understand this natural process, the fear of what is happening is reduced. You will be able to better receive comfort, compassion, and care as the body performs its final task of closing down. The better you understand this natural progression, the less upsetting and alarming it is as you experience death yourself.

The Most Personal Journey

We have been traveling this journey together up to this point and discovered many things about our thoughts and feelings. Now we travel a little further, realizing that this part of our journey is slower and, in some ways, easier as our body knows exactly what to do. Ending-of-days is the ultimate unknown and can only be entered alone. The simplest definition of death is a moment in time at the end of physical life preceded by a dying process.

The Physical Process of Your Body Closing Down

The body closing down is simple, logical, and sequential. Once understood, death can become less demanding and problematic. In some ways this makes dying easier to experience. For others, the fact that this closing down cannot be reversed can still be upsetting. Death arrives when all the body systems stop functioning. Remember this is a normal, sequential, and generally unromantic process, and *not* a medical emergency.

Ending-of-days does *not* require medical intervention. Rather, this is the time to give and receive love, compassion, and comfort measures.

As Your Ending-of-Days Comes Nearer

The body has an amazing ability to cope and adjust to all types of disruptions and imbalances. At first it treats the slowing down of different systems by adjusting, for example: breathing becomes more rapid to offset the decreasing power of the heart to pump blood to all areas of the body. As ending-of-days comes nearer, the body can no longer cope and adjust so it moves into gently beginning to systematically close down.

Mental, Social, and Psychological Changes

This beautiful, yet gentle process of dying begins with a gradual withdrawal from outer world concerns. There is an increasing interest in being comfortable, in having a safe place where your needs are met. Often, there is an increasing need for stillness and quiet. There is little interest in TV, music, or social activities. There is a deepening awareness, a gentle acceptance, and inner understanding of the process. Many discover the ending-of-days can be a time of gentle participation, being awake, aware, and comfortable while living life up to the last breath.

The Last Days

There are many normal changes in these last days as your body closes down beginning in the extremities and slowly progressing to the heart. Once familiar with these changes, comfort measures may be introduced with the result of supporting the body's process and not mistakenly hindering what the body so beautifully knows to do - close down.

Appetite and Dehydration

Appetite is certainly one of the most common concerns of family and friends. The fear of starving you is not reality. It is based on knowing how we feel when we have not eaten for a while, or have been sick. Ending-of-days is a different situation: the body is closing down. The stomach has reduced digestive enzymes and the ability to digest or assimilate foods/liquids is lowered. Plus, the gag reflex is decreasing and swallowing becomes more difficult. As a result, feeding tubes offer no change in quality or quantity of life. *And* once inserted feeding tubes are often difficult to have removed. Because of the irritation on the back of the throat, feeding tubes can even result in a more painful death. This is no longer the preferred method of nutritional support. Physicians now put in a G-Tube that creates an opening directly to the stomach. Either way, the body is still closing down and nourishment is not needed.

In the last hours of the last day, dehydration appears to stimulate the release of natural painkillers called endorphins plus other anesthetic compounds that support a feeling of well-being. In the last days, many often refuse food and liquids as the digestive system continues closing down. This is a normal process that can be supported by simply moistening the lips. At the end-of-days your body is conserving the energy previously

7 — Arriving at Your Destination

used for digestion to be used in supporting other more vital systems. In refusing food, you are not starving or rejecting your loved ones and their offerings; it is simply the body closing down.

About this time intravenous fluids (IVs) are often considered or are already in place. Care needs to be given here since IVs can be supportive of some symptoms, yet your body is closing down in a normal natural way. Your body can no longer handle this excess fluid and this can result in a fluid overload. This in turn may cause both painful edema (swelling) and shortness of breath. Since you have advanced directives, this can usually be avoided. You were smart for doing that.

Wakefulness and Sleep

As ending-of-days approaches you may be spending more time in a sleep-like state with increasing difficulty in being aroused. This is a natural preparation for the transition and is neither a "giving up" nor rejection of your family. Your body has less energy and is turning inward to sustain the most important body functions for as long as possible. Your loved ones need to remember it's okay to allow you to rest. They need to remember that, although you might not be talking, your hearing remains to the last breath. Hearing is the last sense to leave, as it is the final sense of protection though your body is not able to respond.

With decreasing metabolism, you might experience confusion and restlessness as the life energy is withdrawing from the thinking part of your brain. This confusion usually is about who is here physically, while at the same time you may have visions—seeing loved ones who have already passed. At this time, the veil between the physical and spiritual world is very thin. Sometimes, as the ending-of-days draws near, you might have a sudden burst of energy and wakefulness, opening your eyes, and being very clear with the persons with you. This is usually temporary. Loved ones can respond with loving, caressing, and speaking words of release and comfort.

You might seem to be restless or agitated, which appears as repetitive motions such as pulling at the bed linens and clothing. This is due in part to metabolic changes and the decrease of oxygen to your brain. Please know that you are not having *pain* or *distress*. Rather your body is closing down. It is not necessary for anyone or anything to get in the way of the process.

Breathing

With the approaching ending-of-days, your slowed breathing becomes noticeable. Your breaths become further apart and can vary in depth and regularity. This change from a normal breathing pattern usually marks more imminent death. The body is remarkable. By the time these breathing changes occur, you are in the process of leaving your physical body. With the natural endorphins that the body produces, you are not aware of these changes. It's like going out the door of your home and not being aware that a window is open. Gurgling sounds in your chest may become loud. This sound, though distressful to your loved ones, is normal from fluid that does not need to be coughed up as your lungs are closing down. Your loved ones may want you to be suctioned. This is *not* necessary as suctioning usually increases secretions, so it is discouraged.

There are four breathing patterns that may occur as your ending-of-days becomes imminent. These breathing patterns may or may not occur and are in no order of frequency or importance.

7 — Arriving at Your Destination

1. Cheyne – Stokes breathing is shallow breathing then no breathing for approximately five to sixty seconds.
2. Periods of shallow panting. Both of these breathing patterns are related to decreasing blood flow to internal organs. Both are normal and without pain.
3. "Fish out of water" breathing is not often seen and is an exaggerated gulping motion as your lungs and heart are closing down. These are the final reflex actions of the lungs closing down. These breaths become further and further apart until they cease. As such, they are *not* painful, and you do *not* need the oxygen.
4. Breathing continues to slow, becomes shallow and gently stops. This is the *most common* breathing pattern at end of days.
5. Finally, there is the "moment of death," an exhale which is an automatic reflex exhale with no pain. It is the final release and letting go.

A client, describing her father's death, said, "He got up in the morning and went to the bathroom."

On return to bed, he said to his wife, "I feel so heavy."

She replied, "Oh, Ralph, we don't have to get up early to do anything. I'll go to the bathroom and then we can snuggle for a while."

As she entered the door returning from the bathroom, she heard him softly say, "Sara." And he was gone.

One of our friend's oldest daughters is a nurse and lovingly works in ending-of-days. When her grandmother was dying, the daughter came to be with her at night. On the last morning, as the sun was rising, the daughter curled around her grandmother and put her hand on her grandmother's heart, and gently said, "Oh, grandmother, you have been working so hard all night, the daylight is coming and it's okay to leave. You are loved." Grandmother took a final gentle exhale and was gone.

Blood Pressure, Temperature, and Circulation

Wide changes in blood pressure and pulse characterize the last few ending-of-days. The circulation withdrawing from the extremities into the inner organs can sometimes cause emotional outbursts such as anger and grief as the brain's neurons misfire. In the orderly beauty of dying, you are not aware of them.

The temperature of your arms and legs begins to change from very warm to very cold as the regulating mechanism begins to weaken. Mottled or blotchy skin patches begin to appear around your mouth, nose, and extremities as well as on lower body parts such as the back of the buttock, feet, and legs. On your buttock, blotchy skin might be seen when you are turned over onto your side. Skin colors begin to vary from rosy pink to grey blue, or even purple. You are not aware of being cold as you are leaving; your loved ones are and lovingly cover you with a blanket.

As the circulatory system continues to close down, your blood pressure continues to become more erratic in volume, frequency, and intensity. As your heart stops and your blood no longer circulates, your ending-of-days is complete.

Senses

Even your senses adapt, change, and slowly diminish in your ending-of-days. With smell, there is a noticeable decrease in the enjoyment of the aroma of foods. This often causes nausea or an upset stomach. Your taste in food changes and your

7 — Arriving at Your Destination

interest in eating diminishes. Your digestive system is gradually closing down.

Your eyesight diminishes, and your eyes begin to remain open with a glassy stare and an inability to focus on external objects. Your sight is being withdrawn from the outer sensory world.

You might raise your hands up as if reaching for something, then slowly and gently your eyes become more and more glassy and fixed. At this point, your family will know your ending-of-days is within hours.

Your hearing appears to be strong to the very end. Yet, you cannot respond. At this time your family or loved ones will be giving you loving words and farewells.

A nurse friend and her attorney brother were with their mother immediately after a stroke from which she did not regain consciousness. They were sitting on either side of the bed. He was holding her hand and they were reminiscing about funny things that happened to their family that brought them closer together. At one point the brother said, "I think that Mom is trying to connect. Every now and then she twitches her hand." He was disappointed to learn later that this was her nervous system erratically misfiring as it was closing down.

Then, when they were laughing very hard, suddenly their mother raised her right arm straight up into the air. The brother's eyes got big as he looked at his sister. She got up and gently put her mom's hand back down at her side and said, "It's ok, Mom, you don't have to raise your hand to speak . . . it's family."

The important thing for you to remember is that a natural death is possible. The body follows a systematic process of closing down all body functions. Your internal conductor orchestrates the most incredible symphony of closing down that is normal and natural. Usually when relaxed and accepting, one experiences death with no pain. This process was designed to be gentle and almost beautiful in its simplicity. When you are relaxed and accepting you will "go gently into the night."

There are times, however, that acute pain from cancer, organ failure, or other end-stage processes may occur. In these instances, medications, herbals, and energy therapies may be used to relieve the pain and soothe the psyche.

And on The Last Day

And on the last day, death comes unbidden without asking. For each person the ending-of-days has to be entered alone. Loved ones and health professionals can only go to the edge with you. You must enter this transition alone . . . into the "all one."

Death is but a single moment in time.

Your body knew how to create itself beginning with conception. At the moment of your ending-of-days your body begins to "uncreate" itself.

The picture of death, the final closing down of all the body functions, looks something like this:
- the heart stops pumping
- breathing ends
- all muscles relax
- the jaw usually opens slightly
- the eyes remain fixed and dilated

Summary

In the final days of physical life, all systems in your body are systematically closing down. None are exempted. This process is natural, exquisite in its grand design, and experienced by everyone. Once you understand the process, the ending-of-days can begin to take its rightful place in physical life. This phenomenon is one of the most important major events in every one's life, second only to physical birth.

Without death, life itself would have no conclusion, no culmination. To live forever could itself become a dreaded disease. But ending-of-days, alone in the here and now, is not a disease to be treated and fought. Rather, ending of days is a normal natural process we can respond to with love, compassion, comfort measures, dignity, and release.

Remember, you don't have to do anything. Your body knows how to do it all. Isn't that the good news?

> *Hi all my loved ones,*
>
> *I'm really surprised here. I didn't realize how much my body was going to be doing for me. I guess it sounds silly but I'm glad that my body knows what to do because I don't think I could do this. And so much of it happens while I'm just getting ready to pass over and be with Bobby and Aunt Grace… there's so much to be looking forward to. This is going to be* ok. *It really is. I'm so glad I get to know this and share it with you all.*
>
> *Much love and hugs . . .*
>
> *M*

8

The Big "N" — NEXT

That's right. The *big* "N" . . . Next? I have so many questions that I want to know before my ending of days. What happens after my journey ends? Is this where I enter the Great Mystery? What happens to my body? What about my loved ones? Who is taking care of my things I left behind? There are so many questions that I want to know so my family and I can be as ready as we can be . . . .

What Happens After My Journey Ends?

This is a great question and one that really has no answer, because in 99.9 percent of deaths the body has no physical return. Entering the Great Mystery is probably the best name for this physical ending-of-days. Yes, there are stories of people being clinically dead and coming alive again. There are reports of people who talk with the dead but no one knows for sure. There are stories of people across the planet who have awakened upon dying, but no one knows for sure why. There are reports of a deep feeling of peace and a love so deep and gentle that it is beyond knowing. We like the last report the best. No one knows for sure; it certainly is the Great Mystery that is entered alone.

And yet, this is one of the great mysteries of life that religion and sages have alluded to for centuries. The belief in an afterlife where the soul is free of the body already brings much comfort to many people. We have been witnesses to souls crossing over. We have felt and seen the soul leave the body. We find that death is not the victor. There is no sting to the dying. Rather, there is a sacredness, a stillness, that is beyond words. It is an honor and privilege to be present and witness this most sacred of all life's processes.

What Happens to My Body?

In The Last Journey, we are looking at a peaceful, expected death.

- At the time of death, the medical provider on call, house nurse supervisor or hospice nurse records the time of your death, those present, the nature of the death and any important devices in use, signing their name and contact information in the appropriate record.
- Your family may choose to sit with you immediately after the ending-of-days allowing for last goodbyes or stay with you as part of religious customs or cultural/family traditions.
- Family members may wish to assist with your personal care based on individual wishes, religious or cultural requirements. Note: due to some conditions, changes can begin soon after death and are normal, just occasionally accelerated,

aspect of the body decomposing—ashes to ashes, dust to dust.

After your passing, care, dignity, and compassion continue. At each step, health care professionals are mindful that a soul has just left this planet and their sacred task is to honor and respect the body.

These are the assurances underlying how care of your body after death usually occurs:
- honoring the spiritual/cultural wishes of the deceased person and their family while making certain that legal obligations are met
- respectfully preparing the body for transfer to mortuary, funeral home, or the family
- offering the family present the opportunity to participate in the care after death and supporting them to do so
- ensuring the privacy and dignity of the deceased person
- ensuring the health and safety of everyone coming in contact with the body.
- returning deceased person's personal possessions to their relatives

"Who does what?" is the question that most people ask after the death of a loved one. To have some prior knowledge helps your family have a greater sense of control at a time when there is no control of your physical deterioration.

There are many professionals involved in care after death including nurses, doctors, mortuary staff, hospital transport staff, ambulance staff, social services, funeral directors, bereavement counselors, and ministers/priests. Other professionals, depending on the type of death, may include coroners, pathologists, and police. You will never see many of these professionals as they are behind the scenes, yet they are all important for things to run smoothly for you and your family.

What About My Loved Ones After I Am Gone?

This first year of life after your death is quite possibly one of the most challenging life experiences that your loved ones will ever have. It is adjusting to new circumstances, a new lifestyle, perhaps some not so pleasant financial realities. It means living alone for a while or even longer.

If you had a spouse or significant other, you are no longer a couple. You are now single and maybe considered a widow or a widower. Widow or widower—now those are words you don't hear much anymore. And none of these labels really fit on any official form that you might fill out.

You, as the survivor, will have many adjustments with friends, family, and others who have always viewed you as part of an inseparable pair; so much so that your names were said together so often, you thought of yourselves as a shared identity. One widow described it as now being half a pair of scissors. And, if you are single with no family, then it is those closest friends that will have many adjustments to make.

If you were a parent, your adult children also face a similar dilemma. Our western culture does not really speak to this transition. Rather the expectation after a funeral is to get on with life or your mother/father was sick or old. So, what did you expect?" For many, the final passage to adulthood is the loss of their parents.

Often children will feel responsible for the surviving parent. These are new feelings along with new responsibilities that make this journey even more special. They will experience both grief for the loss of a parent and the changing role/status of the remaining parent. Often, it's challenging for adult children to begin seeing the surviving parent as a unique and *capable* person. Their desire to "help" can quickly become micromanaging, albeit well-intentioned.

The first year after your passing becomes a new journey for those left behind that begins with, "How can I ever live without . . . ?" Very simply, you can and you will. This is a journey of learning to be *alone* but not *lonely*.

Consider the word alone; divided it becomes "all one." The Old English origin is literally "wholly oneself." Perhaps this meaning is a "way shower" to something more than ourselves, The All of the All, a unity with the most holy. Shifting your perception just slightly can shift the word into a pointer of something more than your physical body where there is all-inclusion, peacefulness, and the calm in the midst of the storm of emotions.

Your loved ones will discover taking their new life one day at a time and sometimes it's one breath at a time. In life, we always have a choice as to how we approach every situation, every change, every adjustment. One option is to contract, resist, and go through this time with grit and determination. A second option is to choose to expand and "grow through" this new experience. The option of "growing through" suggests openness to discovery and learning to live with grace, flow, ease, and eventually acceptance. Hopefully your loved ones will choose to "grow through" your loss.

Allowing the Presence of Grief

Everyone responds to the loss of a loved one in their own way and in their own time. There is no magic bullet here. There may be times when one feels calm and peaceful, "in control" and "strong." Other times one feels sad, weepy, angry, or out of control. Swings in emotions can feel intense and sometimes raw. This journey is one of growth and rebalancing oneself after the shock of the death. Yes, it's a shock even when you know it is coming. There is a part of us that wants to believe that this is a dream, or some miracle will happen. The simple truth is death is a part of the physical life cycle of all living plants, animals, the planet, and even the solar system.

For many, these are difficult words to read and accept; for others these words bring comfort in the natural cycle of life. Dog lovers will appreciate this story. When six years old, a gentleman in Georgia knew that his dog, Lady, was old and that she was having trouble walking. He was in disbelief that the doctor couldn't fix her and she died. It was his first experience with death. He had parents who gently helped him accept the truth and remember all the fun times they had together. They buried Lady in the woods, where she liked to run in a shady spot that his daddy said a deer had slept in the night before. He knew that Lady would be warm.

What we know from personal experience, and the experiences of others, is that on this life plane, grief is seen as a natural, normal process. All animals grieve for different amounts of time. Great Northern geese mate for life. When one goose dies, the mate stays by its side unless someone or something removes the body. Mallard ducks in contrast are frantic for maybe thirty seconds when one of their goslings is pulled under the water by a turtle, but then slow down and swim away.

8 — The Big "N" NEXT

We have been taught that as much as it hurts and as hard as it seems to breathe or to get through a day, grief must be felt to be released. This may be true, or it may not. Is it possible for grief to be felt in a safe loving environment that allows the grief to open and then slowly dissolve into the love that surrounds it? Does that sound or feel interesting? Are you curious? What if you could become the Watcher, become the loving space or environment around the grief?

Becoming the Watcher

You can try it now. Sit in a quiet place where you won't be disturbed. Close your eyes and breathe slowly in and out. Feel your gentle breathing for several moments or longer. Now think of a situation that you have experienced where you didn't like the outcome, or you felt angry and upset. See yourself stepping back from it so you are here, and the situation is in front of you.

Gently smile and continue your slow gentle breathing and surround the situation with a soft, gentle cloud of love. Continue breathing and smiling. You are bringing love and peace to the situation. Continue to breathe and being in the love and peace.

Watch and feel the anger and upset slowly expand and dissolve into the surrounding love.

Remain in that gentle breathing until all that is left is love and peace.

Gently open your eyes and enjoy the overall peace in your body and mind. Smile and give thanks for the releasing. Gently return to your breathing for a brief time then when you are ready, gently go about your day. You may repeat being the watcher any time that you are upset and/or angry about a situation.

The Watcher

You become the watcher of your grief rather than getting lost in its embrace. As the observer, you have taken yourself out of the picture and gently surrounded the emotion with love and gentle soft breathing. You can use this in any unhappy or angry situation. This is a very powerful, yet simple process that enables you to release anything that is not supportive of your well-being.

Dealing with one's profound emotions might seem at first to be frightening. However, this is a way that you can acknowledge and honor your grief by allowing it to express itself in a loving and caring space. As you embrace your grief and allow it to be, it will begin to shift and change. You may journey with your emotions repeatedly as necessary as the intensity begins to lessen. Smile and notice the subtle shift that is beginning to take place as you start to step back and watch.

As you become the "watcher" of your emotions rather than a "victim" lost in your emotions, you begin to discover a deeper peace often called "the peace that surpasses all understanding." It begins to radiate from the empty inner space created by loss and spreads across your entire body filling you. This is often a gradual process, an unconscious move towards a fulfilling life without a loved one. You find you are beginning to embrace life again.

Your loved ones will always remember you, their loved one. They never forget, rather the pain of loss is transmuted into cherishing and honoring the time you had together.

When the Tears Come

Some people cry on the outside, some cry on the inside. Some people cry a lot; some cry a little. Some do not cry. Yet, they are all right where they need to be in their process. At times it seems as if the tears will never stop or perhaps, they will never come. Tears become your emotions way of trying to adjust to the hole in the fabric of life that death has created.

Emotional tears, such as with a death of a loved one, heal the heart by returning your family to their hearts. Crying makes your loved ones feel better even though they are not better nor is the situation getting better. As such, crying is essential to grief when the waves of tears occasionally overcome those who survive. Tears assist your loved ones to process your passing so they can keep living with open hearts. Tears feel very cleansing and a way to purge pent up emotions, so they don't get "stuck" in the body as stress, pain, or fatigue.

Your family's tears for your loss will ebb over time only to return at strange moments or at events that trigger memories. Tears are natural grief being expressed and part of the journey. Tears are the key to disperse the cobwebs of the mind and release them deeper into the mysterious depths of their hearts. Yes, tears will fall and relieve your loved ones of their mental stress and negative thinking. Be glad they are falling.

One grandmama shared that when she was sad and crying, she said, "When things get so bad, I cry, but when my tears are dry, I go into action." This is true and this is how it works. Tears are a cleansing process that will gradually begin to open your loved ones up to living in the moment and moving into a new life. Sadness and grief will lessen over time for your family and friends. They will begin to look for ways to remember, cherish and be thankful for the time that they had with you.

The Power of Your Breath to Assist You, the Traveler

It's time to take a break from your reading. It's time to regroup and refresh. One of the easiest and fastest ways is to breathe . . . That's right, breathe. When we get tired or stressed, our breath becomes shallow or we even hold our breath. So, let's stop and *breathe*. Take three slow easy breaths right *now*.

The breath is our closest and constant companion. This is the time to use it and use it often. When we get tired, upset, or uncomfortable, our first unconscious reaction is to stop breathing. We become alert and aware. This is our fight or flight mechanism stepping in to see what is needed. When we are breathing normally, we are relaxed. So, let's practice being in a relaxed state before we need it.

Simply focus on your breathing. Feel the cool air going in and the warm air coming out. Keep focusing on the breath and close your eyes or move into a soft gaze. This simple act allows the tears and anger to emerge from within without hindrance. It gives the body a mechanism to express emotions. Sometimes you might forget to breathe when a wave of feelings comes over you, that's okay. Simply return to the breath when you remember. Time and practice make this an effective "habit" or response to tears and is a feeling of healthy letting go. Be gentle with yourself.

Ok, now some slow easy breaths before we move on to another topic. Sometimes it is helpful to get up and move around. Sitting more than twenty minutes can dull our senses and even make us feel sleepy. So, get up, stretch, and smile.

Hi there,

Just a quick note. I'm feeling a lot better in a good way knowing what will happen to my body after my end of days. I find that very comforting. Wait and see—you will too. Plus knowing that you all will be ok gives me much peace of mind. I don't mind leaving.

Love you,
M

8 — The Big "N" NEXT

What Happens to the Things I Left Behind?

Hopefully you have taken the time at some point on this Last Journey to make a list of all your important things and to whom you want to leave them. If not, that's okay if you want your family and/or friends to make the decisions. However, it is best and creates fewer hard feelings if you make a list before you die.

Better yet, when a friend or loved one comes to visit, send them home with something you want them to have. When giving away an heirloom or something of value or significance, be sure to share the history of the item and all the memories connected to it.

Giving Away and Reorganizing

Giving away and reorganizing takes many forms. There is no rush here. Your family can take their time and move to their own rhythm. They will probably discover that this is their sacred time of remembering and putting away memories and gently closing another door.

Home Death

If you had a home death, your spouse or loved one who shared the bedroom and the house will decide what to do. Some desire to immediately move the furniture, especially if there is a hospital bed or other medical equipment that needs to be removed. Others prefer to leave the bedroom or other spaces just as they were. Often a favorite chair or desk serves as a lovely memory.

A friend keeps her husband's favorite sweater on a hanger in the closet they shared. His scent still clings to the sweater and is a reminder of his presence in her life.

As with so many decisions in life, there is seldom a right or wrong. It is simply a choice that makes your loved ones more comfortable. This is often challenging and difficult to anticipate. Hopefully they will take their time and not be rushed. Consider making three piles: keep, release, and I don't know. You can easily guess which pile has the most things.

Again, take frequent breaks, as this can be stressful and tiring. And, as we just learned, part of the stress response is to slow or stop breathing. Interestingly, as one gets tired, even more goes into the "I don't know pile." Remember even if only one hanger is removed, it is a start. It is not how much is accomplished, but that progress is being made. This is not a race and there is no reward. How do you know what to keep? Good question. That object goes into the "I don't know pile." One never knows when that hammer or pocket watch might prove useful.

The Last Time

Within the giving away and reorganizing there is the ritual of "last time." These actions are often a gentle realization that life is different now, and thus begins a gentle closing of the past. A friend called some days after her husband's passing to say that she finally did the laundry. She paused and said sadly, "This is the last time that I will wash Philip's clothes."

Other discoveries, such as finding tools, books, or old photos create similar emotions, often with laughter or tears, but always with memories of you, their loved one. With the realization of absence comes another step in their healing.

Giving away your personal possessions can take place quickly, be done incrementally in the first year, or over a longer period. Giving away items like clothes, shoes, and jewelry is often healing as it signals that on some level your loved ones are acknowledging the finality of loss. Often, the process begins with the more generic possessions and gradually moves into the more intimate objects with special meaning like tickets to a favorite movie shared together or a special dress or aftershave.

One middle-aged woman shared this story on the death of her father. Even though she was smaller than her dad, she wore his large plaid winter jacket for the first winter. Doing so brought her a feeling of comfort and reassurance that all was well. The second winter, the coat was not needed and she donated it to a "winter coat drive for the cold" with the feeling that now it was time to have someone else enjoy the warmth it offered. Sharing items with children and grandchildren can also provide a special memento and become a treasured heirloom.

At Christmas, a dear friend gave each of her adult granddaughters a gift of jewelry that their recently deceased grandfather had given her. After carefully selecting a specific piece for each of the young women, she wrote on a card the history and significance of each piece and included it with the gift. It was her hope that by sharing these treasured items, they would become cherished heirlooms for her granddaughters and help them remember the grandfather (and grandmother) who loved them.

Holiday Celebrations

During the first year after your death, the holidays can bring sadness and sometimes pain as memories arise about how it used to be and will never be again. Seasonal events, birthdays, anniversaries, and family gatherings can be occasions to create new rituals that are life enhancing, honoring you while easing the pain of loss and accompanying feelings. It is a "bittersweet" time when your family and friends can reminisce and treasure memories about you.

Celebrations can take many forms. One mom chose to celebrate her husband's date of passing with a "Rebirth into Spirit" celebration complete with a rebirthday cake, a rebirthday song, and a toast. The family meal was filled with laughter as they chose to remember the great times and wisdom of their dad.

Another family spent their first Christmas without their grandmother, who had lived with them, by taking a walk in the forest behind their home where she spent many hours. They recalled her favorite stories about nature and watched for her favorite elves and woodland creatures.

Other survivors create new traditions as continuing the old morphs into a new place in their memory and allows for creating new memories. Taking a trip to a new location or trying something new is a way to recognize there is a new chapter in the journey of life.

Remembering

Remembering is a healthy aspect of life, recalling the good times and the not so good times. We recall things from our childhood and youth that are triggered by present events. As your family begins to unpack their memories, this can be very healing.

At first your family and loved ones will be filled with memories of what it was like then and what it is like now—the loss, the hole that has been opened in their life. This is normal and natural. Over time their memories soften as the sting of loss begins to fade. Memories may arise from a special food, a song, a special place or even a sunset. If they stay with the emotion, it can become a special moment; even a bittersweet one.

Some family members become the watcher of the emotion rather than becoming immersed in the emotion. For example, watch how an emotional pain can spread to the cells of your body. Being the watcher, continue to breathe with this process consciously as you become the watcher. Trust that your breath and your body know exactly what to do, which they do. As we embrace the memory it can be treasured or dissipated. Irrespective of choice, we create room for peace to emerge. This is a simple exercise that you can also do with good results.

There is no right or wrong way to remember. It is in remembering that your family honors your life and you.

Please be aware that not all remembering is positive; sometimes our loved ones dwell on or engage in past grievances and offenses. Such focus on negative events can get in their way of grieving and moving on with life's journey.

Many religious traditions call for forgiveness as a first step in healing the spirit. They all point to the same thing. As one first forgives themselves, their self-imposed shackles are set free. As your loved ones go through the same process, they discover that it is very liberating and essential to a healthy life after the loss of a loved one such as you.

Maintaining Hope and Faith

Your loved ones' own hope and faith that comes from things not seen are what sustains them until they once again know and feel whole and safe. Maintaining hope and faith comes in many shapes and forms. These emotions are often not shared nor talked about by family and friends since they might be seen as odd or strange.

One lady had a sense that her late husband was talking with her when she sat in his favorite chair. So, she got out a notebook and asked him questions, first about what to do and then more about what it was like where he was. She wrote everything down for many months. Then their daily times together became more erratic as she increasingly became involved with life again. Soon, she talked with him when she needed a little extra comfort. Ten years later she remembers how much that transition time was a period of comfort, hope, and faith that she could go on without him.

You might find your deceased loved ones talking with you. This is not uncommon. Most people don't talk about it or only in a whisper to a close friend or confidant. After the death of his wife, a Texas gentleman would nightly walk the mile long road from his ranch to the highway and talk with her amidst the starry night. On the walk out he talked; on the return walk he simply allowed himself to connect with the immensity of the universe and he could feel her love surround him.

Another woman, upon the loss of her husband of many years, would feel his warmth and presence as she fell asleep each night. And still, another woman created a ritual of walking down to the lake like they did to watch the sunset and feel the connectedness with all nature. She would talk to the setting sun and feel connected to her husband and all of creation giving her insight, peace, and wisdom.

Getting Stuck and Unstuck

For many loved ones, their grief has a gentle flow as loss turns into cherishing the time together. For others, loss seems to become built into the fabric of their personality and they don't know how to let it go. Sadly, the loss has replaced their loved one, *and*—if they did let it go—they would let go of their loved one and perhaps not be able to move on. It is as if moving on somehow diminishes the memories of the loved one. Hopefully, that's not true of your loved ones.

This is a tough place to be as "stuckness" is hard to verbalize, but your loved ones will know when they have it. It may be periodic; however, it is still possible to let go of the loss, cherish you in their heart, and live a full life again.

Your extended family may be watching and wanting to help, but feel at a loss as to what to do. Hopefully, your immediate family is able to ask for help from other family members, friends, or health professionals. This may be difficult but is usually beneficial. Often it is the only way to get "unstuck."

Is it possible to let go of the hurt, cherish your precious loved one in your heart, and live a full life again? That's a discovery question we leave for your loved ones. Only they can discover the answer, one breath at a time.

What Happens the First Year After My Passing?

After the first year of your passing, the anniversary date will be remembered and often celebrated or thought of year after year. This is the start of closing a door on saying goodbye. Your loved ones probably will feel a softening around your loss and recognize that you really are gone from their sight. Remember that you are never lost or forgotten, rather you remain always deep within them, whatever the emotion they are feeling. Even years after your death, a song, a picture, or something unexpected can evoke a soft response of remembering you.

A Rite of Passage

The first-year rituals are, in many ways, a rite of passage for your loved ones to go on with their lives, finding meaning and purpose. The gentle closures along the way are small wins that pave the way for a gentle re-entry into moving into the next phase of their lives. *And*, if you were alive, this is exactly what you would want for them—to live and grow and move on with their lives and be happy.

> *Dear family and friends,*
>
> *I feel better knowing that you will be okay. I know that's important for you to have times of both sadness and happiness. Remember how I was after my sister died unexpectedly? I was up and down for a while but then I just began to be more content and accepting. Couldn't change that one. I'm so glad I got to think about how important that first year is for you.*
>
> *I love you all,*
> *M*

9

There's No Such Place as Faraway

Here you are at the completion of your road map and embarking on your special one-of-a-kind Last Journey. It is an ending, and with all endings there is a beginning. We know that nothing lasts forever. You see this all the time. Tomato seeds are planted; they grow and are eaten; vines are cut down and composted. This is an example of impermanence.

Every living thing has an ending-of-days. And now that you see how unique each moment is, you can begin to appreciate the richness of each day and each breath as being a one-of-a-kind, never to be repeated. Although many days may look like the previous ones you now know they are not.

There are both obvious and subtle differences that you may pick up with your senses. The sun casts different shadows on a cloudy day; the smell after a rain feels fresh and "clean." Your food tastes better when prepared with love. You might hear subtle sounds more clearly as you allow silence to be your friend. Sitting on the front porch or on your deck becomes a symphony of sounds and movement as you become increasingly in sync with nature.

When you take the time to be still and enjoy the moment, you enlarge your sense awareness. You begin to listen with your body and allow yourself to be more comfortable with being still. There is a gently increasing awareness of the connectedness that is both comforting and relaxing. Many of us have seen this in our parents or relatives in the last couple of years before their ending-of-days. Although up and engaged, there were times of pausing when they seemed far away and briefly at peace, then they would reengage.

When one lady asked her mother about this, her mother said, "This must be the peace that surpasses understanding" that she could be here and there at the same time. It was like time and space were collapsing into being here now.

So that brings us to the question: if there is no such place as far away, then where are we really? Is it possible to be here now in any place in time and space? We call this is a "discovery question." That means there is no "yes" or "no" answer; rather each of us discovers the answer for ourselves.

What we do know is that where you focus your attention is where you are. If you focus it on the past, you are there. Similarly, if you focus on the future, you can be there. If you focus on a daughter or friend, you are there. And, if you focus on someone who is far away or someone who has passed, you are with them. Think about it like this . . . you know your friend is at work and you can't get in touch with him. You can still think about him and feel his comfort or discomfort. The same goes for our loved ones who have died. Just because you cannot see them doesn't mean they are not there!

This is one of the most common questions when working with newly widowed persons or parents who have lost a child, or on airplanes when our traveling companions discover we are in the health care field and work in ending-of-days. "I can still feel his/her Presence with me." This is probably the major topic in the physical life-death continuum that is rarely addressed or talked about among many people.

Yet, this "felt" Presence could be the most important part as it brings great comfort and support to those still on the physical plane. The veil between the two worlds becomes very thin at the time of death. There is a slow disconnection—a physiological process that continues in the theorized "vibrational state" for the first forty-five days after the passing. When your loved ones embrace and talk about it, the better you all are. We all go through this process. And yet sadly, this natural process and "felt" Presence is rarely talked about or commonly known. It's like if you don't talk about death and dying, then somehow death and dying will go away or you don't have to deal with it. The exact opposite is true.

The felt Presence of someone who has passed is one of many discovery questions for your loved ones to explore and discover what their truth is. Truth is truth even if we do not choose to accept it.

A final thought to consider; knowing someone you love is going to die provides you a rare opportunity to live each day with them as if it is their last. What would you do if you knew this was your last day to live? How would your life be different? Would you spend more time talking with your loved ones? Hugging them? Saying thank you? Enjoying a great meal? Taking that sunset walk you love so much? Hugging your dog or cat? Being in deep gratitude, what would you do differently?

The bottom line is no one knows when they are going to die. It could be today. Life is so unsure of even the immediate future. So why wait, why not live each day as if it was your last? Think about it. What a great day that would be—full of love, beauty, joy, hugs, and deep gratitude. Isn't that what we all want any way? Why wait? Begin today.

You are mortal and you are going to die. What if your needs and desires had nothing to do with your age? What if your needs and desires were simply your personal sense of how finite your time is? Think about how much that would simplify decisions. The questions of when and what to fix in/on your body become one question, "Do I fix it or not?"

Do you really want to sacrifice your quality of living with surgeries, chemotherapy, and/or intensive care for a "chance" of gaining a little time? Is the cost of your happiness too high on a chance? Rather, what if we all focused on having the fullest and richest time now? We're talking about being free of pain, maintaining mental awareness and clarity for as long as possible, laughing and celebrating the richness of life right now, and being able to be with our family and/or loved ones.

There is a Zen saying, "You live longer only when you stop trying to live longer." It's the old "trying trick." Try to pick up your pen. No, don't pick it up. *Try* to pick it up. You cannot. Trying is not doing.

Have you ever thought about listening with your heart? What makes you smile, feel happy? What makes your heart sing? These are the things that you need to be doing. These are the priorities to do *now*. Oftentimes, we put things off until the dishes are done, the clothes are folded, the lawn mowed, or the children finish school. Living life this way, we may miss the sunset, the dog playing with its tail, and the ice cream truck coming down the street.

Many have said that your heart is your connection to your soul. It's like the bridge between this world and the next world. The more you listen to your heart, the happier, the more content and the more peaceful you can become. Remember, the heart can only beat in the present moment. Listening to your heart can only occur in the present moment. Life is only lived in the present moment.

Being here now means that every moment becomes alive, full of rich sense awareness. Being here now, experiencing this moment and doing what really matters opens the opportunity to experience life fresh and new. Everything becomes a thing of joy and a new experience of discovery. It's like all our "things" take on new meaning as we see them as if for the first time and marvel at their beauty, detail, smell, and/or shape.

The message of this book has been one of joy in the moment and discovering that life is to be lived now. Life is to be lived until your last breath. Is this possible? You will see. We all will see.

Our Last Message for You

Our wish is for your increasing comfort with your ending-of-days. We have shared the truth about how life's passing may proceed with love, celebration, and gratitude. We want you to live each day to its fullest experiencing truth, joy, and forgiveness.

Life is a gift. Enjoy and cherish each moment.

Carole Ann
Lynn
Penney

*Some people want to live a long time.
The time to live is right now!*

About the Authors

Carole Ann, and Lynn, are RN, PhDs, and Penney, PhD, educated are professional friends, and colleagues. Together and apart, this trio has traveled life's road experiencing professionally and personally, the transitioning of the human soul into the hereafter. They know and deeply appreciate the scope and depth of living and dying. Throughout their careers each has worked with many ending-of-days patients, clients, and groups both contributing to and learning about the process as they helped others face their own special Last Journey.

Carole Ann Drick, RN, PhD, AHN-BC

Carole Ann's life's work in quality of life began in assisting natural childbirth then morphing into ending-of-days care. Internationally recognized for expertise in Holistic Nursing, self-care and ending-of-days care, she is Director of Conscious Awareness in Austintown, Ohio. With aging parents Carole Ann discovered her innate ability to assist peaceful transitions in person and long distance. Her deep concern for quality of life at ending-of-days is reflected in four books, numerous professional publications, and two American Journal of Nursing Book of the Year Awards.

Lynn Keegan, RN, PhD, AHN-BC, FAAN, GAHN

As an internationally recognized integrative, holistic, nursing pioneer, Lynn is known for her contributions to develop and advance holistic nursing and end-of-life care. She is Director of Holistic Nursing Consultants, Port Angeles, Washington, and Carmel, Indiana and has authored or co-authored twenty-three books and contributed many textbook chapters, articles, and scores of professional journal publications as well as presenting keynote addresses throughout the world. She is a seven-time recipient of the prestigious American Journal of Nursing Book of the Year Award.

K. Penney Sanders, PhD, CPGC

Penney spent over forty years in education including serving as Kentucky's first director of the Office of Education Accountability. Upon her "retirement" she began a 3rd Act of life and became an elder advocate and Certified Professional Guardian in Washington. She taught university courses in research design, public school finance and guardianship while creating her own business serving as an elder advocate. Eleven years later, she remains active in her advocacy work, making the sacred ending-of-days journey many times with her clients.

www.ingramcontent.com/pod-product-compliance
Lightning Source LLC
LaVergne TN
LVHW020437070526
838199LV00063B/4767